VISIONS OF SUGARPLUMS

anne Cullen tormey
3rd of december 1981
cleveland, ohio

Other books by Mimi Sheraton

City Portraits
The Seducer's Cookbook
The German Cookbook
From My Mother's Kitchen

As historical food consultant:

The Horizon Cookbook: An Illustrated History of Eating and Drinking Through the Ages

Illustrations by
Pat Stewart

Mimi Sheraton

VISIONS OF SUGARPLUMS

REVISED AND EXPANDED EDITION

A Cookbook of Cakes, Cookies, Candies, & Confections from All the Countries That Celebrate Christmas

1817

HARPER & ROW, PUBLISHERS, New York
Cambridge, Philadelphia, San Francisco
London, Mexico City, São Paulo, Sydney

The recipe for Martha Washington's Great Cake originally appeared in *The American Heritage Cookbook and Illustrated History of American Eating and Drinking,* © 1964 by American Heritage Publishing Co., Inc. Reprinted by permission.

Recipes for Shaker Christmas Pudding, Excellent Pudding Sauce, and Christmas Bread and Butter Pudding are from *The Shaker Cookbook* by Caroline B. Piercy, © 1953 by Caroline B. Piercy; reprinted by permission of Crown Publishers, Inc.

 For information address Harper & Row, Publishers, Inc., 10 East 53rd Street, New York, N.Y. 10022. Published simultaneously in Canada by Fitzhenry & Whiteside Limited, Toronto.

Designed by Lydia Link

Library of Congress Cataloging in Publication Data

Sheraton, Mimi.
Visions of sugarplums.
Includes index.
1. Christmas cookery. 2. Cookery, International.
I. Title.
TX739.S43 1981 641.5'68 80-7597
ISBN 0-06-014036-4 AACR2

81 82 83 84 85 10 9 8 7 6 5 4 3 2

Contents

Preface to the Revised and Expanded Edition

When this book was first published thirteen years ago, it represented the results of what might be considered a hobby—a joint interest in Christmas and in food that had led me to collect recipes for traditional Christmas confections over many years.

Now that there is a growing interest in nostalgia and what also seems to be an increased concern with tradition and spiritual values in varied forms, it seemed appropriate to expand this collection of highly specialized, highly traditional foods.

Throughout history, various foods have become symbols that nourish the spirit even as they do the body—soul foods, in fact, at their most elemental. Some symbolic foods have become part of formal religious ceremonies, such as the bread and wine of the Eucharist and the church-blessed bread that is an essential feature of the Eastern Orthodox and Central European Easter observances. But most symbolic foods have become part of the lore of folk custom; and similar symbols often have similar meanings in many parts of the world. Beans are considered lucky on New Year's Day in our own South, in the Caribbean and in parts of the Middle East. Grain has symbolized good fortune and plenty from the Roman era, when a loaf of bread was broken over the head of new brides and grooms as part of the marriage ceremony, down to our own time, when bridal couples are showered with rice.

No holiday has a wider variety of special symbolic foods than Christmas, and anyone who prepares the cakes, cookies, candies and drinks related to that holiday can feel a long connection with the past, for many of the foods maintain traditions that began centuries ago—some even before Christianity itself.

A number of recipes in this new edition have been revised, and, I trust, improved, a result of my own changing tastes in the intervening years. But the most important addition is Chapter Nine, containing recipes from friends, most of whom are professional cooks or bakers. Each has generously given me Christmas recipes that are personal favorites and I am grateful to them all: Giuliano Bugialli, John Clancy, Dieter Schorner, Maurice Bonté, Guy Pascal, Charles Patteson, Leon Lianides, and André Soltner.

I must also thank Rena and Gary Coyle, two superb young bakers who did the laborious job of testing and retesting, and who made helpful suggestions throughout. I am indebted to the late Eleanor Lowenstein of the Corner Book Shop in New York, for her help with research on the original edition, and to Hallmark Cards, Inc. for allowing me to use so much of the research I originally did for the exhibition "Bread and Wine," held in the Hallmark Gallery. I am also grateful to the many friends who gave me recipes for the original edition, and whose contributions are repeated here.

M.S.

Introduction

THE SIX WEEKS OF CHRISTMAS

From Advent to Twelfth Night

The birth of Christ is observed at the time of the winter solstice, when the sun leaves the lowest point in the sky and begins to climb higher in the heavens, bringing us longer days—the time when "the light lengthens and the cold strengthens." Like the pagan festivals that preceded it, Christmas celebrates the triumph of light over darkness, promising hope in the midst of despair. In the same way, the Christmas feasting represents one long splurge of luxurious eating, meant to sustain us through the last bitter lap of winter, the Lent of deprivation for which we are rewarded with rebirth and the springtime of Easter.

No Christmas memory would seem to be complete without recollections of the holiday foods, most especially the sweets: the yeasty coffee breads golden with saffron and mace; the aged and ripened fruit cakes spiked with whiskey or brandy and jeweled with bits of candied fruits; crisp butter cookies peppery with ginger or aromatic with anise; darkly rich mince pies, plum cakes and puddings; the flaming wine punches and soul-warming wassails; the sensuously sweet taffies and marzipan candies; and the pervasive, comfortable scents of vanilla, peppermint, nutmeg, cinnamon and cloves.

Golden goose, regal boar's head and chestnut-stuffed turkey notwithstanding, the sweets are the most exciting and imaginative foods of Christmas, and the most symbolic. In addition, they are served not only for one big family dinner but are offered to guests throughout the season.

Since both food and Christmas are two of my most enduring obsessions, I have been collecting these recipes for many years. I have tried to include only those with a special significance at Christmas. Many, such as macaroons, panettone, marzipan and gingerbread, are eaten at other times of the year, but they have always been most particularly identified with Christmas feasting. In much the same way, I have tried to exclude foods that are thought of as festive and so are prepared at this season, just as we might serve caviar as an elegant appetizer at Christmas dinner although it has no special meaning on that day.

Many of the recipes in this book relate directly to the Christmas legend, while others go further back to more ancient observances. Among these are the Scots shortbread, a descendant of the Celtic oat bannock; the plum pudding, said to have been first prepared by a Druid priest in the shadow of the Stonehenge monoliths; the German Springerle cookies, originally honoring the Nordic god Wotan and his horse; the yule log cakes that remind us of the Viking yule log which was burned to chase King Frost from the frozen countryside.

Not only people but animals and invisible spirits are fed at this season, usually on Christmas Eve. In Sweden, huge sheaves of grain are placed outside as edible Christmas trees for birds, while in Southern France, "church bread" is given to animals in their stalls. In Poland and the Ukraine, whole-wheat porridge is set out to placate Father Frost and keep him from destroying crops, while additional porridge is left on the table to feed the spirits of departed relatives, should they return on that evening. In Denmark, a dish of rich rice porridge is placed in the attic for the Julenissen, or Christmas elves, and in many countries, cookies, candies or other foods are left near the fireplace for Santa Claus, should he get hungry on his appointed rounds.

Christmas is in the air not only during the poetic twelve days, but for a full six weeks. The mood sets in religiously, socially, commercially and gastronomically four weeks before Christmas on Advent Sunday, and continues through until January 6th, Twelfth Night. And between those dates are a number of saints' days, each with its own celebrations, observances and foods.

Following is a brief description of the holidays that fall within this six-week period and which are referred to in this book:

Advent begins on the fourth Sunday preceding Christmas and celebrates the coming of Christ into the world. It is a time of Christmas preparations, and in Germany, the traditional time for the holiday baking. Throughout Northern Europe, Advent calendars telling the story of the Nativity are favorites with children, and wreaths of green with big red candles hang in windows and over dining tables. Apple candelabra, such as the one shown here, are also used during Advent in Germany and Scandinavia. In England, the last Sunday before Advent was known as "Stir-Up" Day because the church Collect for that day began with those words and seemed to be a timely reminder to housewives to "stir-up" the mixture for the holiday plum pudding.

December 4th, St. Barbara's Day, is celebrated in many parts of Europe, but most especially in the Levant, where it ushers in the Christmas season. It honors the young and generous girl who shared her bread with the poor in defiance of her father's wishes. Grain is the symbol of the day, and is used as a table decoration in Southern France; it is also served in Lebanon and Syria.

December 6th and 7th, St. Nicholas' Eve and Day, are observed in many countries of Europe, but most especially in Southern Germany, Austria and Holland. It honors the generous fourth-century Bishop Nicholas, also known to Dutch children as Sinterklaas, who visits them with his dark, demonic underworld servant Black Peter. If the children have been good, the shoes they have out in front of the fireplace are filled with candies and cakes. If they have been bad, Black Peter leaves switches and coals. This is the gala celebration of the season in Holland, Christmas itself being a more sober, churchgoing day. In Germany and Austria, children are visited by two relatives or friends, one dressed as the good Nicolo in white robes and a crown, the other all in black, as Krampus. Children report on their behavior in the past year and are fittingly rewarded. Figures of Krampus made of wired prunes and of Nicolo made of figs and marshmallows are favorite decorations in homes and shop windows, the more popular being the mischievous Krampus.

December 13th, St. Lucia's Day, is especially important in Sweden, where it marks the beginning of the Yuletide celebrations. It commemorates the fourth-century Sicilian girl who gave her dowry to impoverished Christians, thus arousing the anger of her suitor, who denounced her as a Christian, thus causing her martyrdom. Early on the morning of December 13th, the prettiest girl in the village or family dresses in a long white robe, and with a crown of burning candles in her hair, wakes the town or household (or guests in a hotel) with coffee and fragrant golden saffron buns—a legend of largesse similar to that of St. Barbara.

December 24th, Christmas Eve or Vigil: Every country has its special Christmas Eve rituals, most of which revolve around the midnight Mass. In France, this evening is known as Réveillon, and after the Mass a large and elegant supper is served, complete with the rich chocolate roll called Bûche de Noël. In Provence, it is customary to offer thirteen sweets as the dessert course. When a premidnight dinner is served, meat is forbidden, and dishes such as eel and dried salt cod in Italy and the similar *lutfisk* in Sweden are traditional. One of the most elaborate Christmas Eve celebrations is the Polish Wigilia, when the first food eaten is the transparent rice wafer, the Oplatekt, that has been blessed and distributed by the parish priest to be broken in bits and served at home. At the Wigilia dinner it is customary to have an even number of dishes and an odd number of guests, allowing one extra place for the Holy Spirit.

December 25th, Christmas Day: The day declared officially to be the birthday of Christ by proclamation of Pope Julius I in the year 350, although historians believe that Jesus was born at a different season. December 25th was chosen because it was the time of the winter solstice, traditionally the season of the Roman Saturnalia, a convenient festival which the Pope knew could easily be adapted to a Christian observance.

December 26th, Boxing Day: In England, this is the day on which gifts are given to house servants and tradesmen. The name refers to the boxes in which the gifts are put. Boxing Day Cake is the traditional recipe for this day. December 26th is also **St. Stephen's Day,** honoring the first Christian martyr and the patron saint of horses—a festival which is an interesting throwback to pagan horse rituals celebrated at this season.

December 31st and January 1st, New Year's Eve and Day: As referred to throughout this book, it is a part of the Christmas cycle, which is why the observances of non-Christian countries were omitted. This was the day of Christ's circumcision, and so is a religious holiday. On this day Greeks celebrate the Feast of St. Basil (St. Vassily) with a handsome braided bread, while in Germany and Central Europe, December 31st is St. Sylvester's Eve and is observed with flaming punches and with an anything-goes free-for-all between the hours of 12 midnight and 1 A.M.

January 6th —known alternatively as **Three Kings' Day** or **Night,** the **Feast of the Magi, Twelfth Night** or **Epiphany**—commemorates the day on which the Three Wise Men brought gifts to the Christ Child. The Eastern church long observed this as the most important day in the Christmas cycle, and many countries still celebrate the day with gift-giving. Yeast breads are the specialties, and usually contain a single almond, bean or china doll as a token of good fortune or to indicate the king and queen of the Twelfth Night revelries.

SWEET YEAST BREADS & COFFEECAKES

Chapter One

The pretzel shape (the baker's sign in Scandinavia) has particular significance at Christmas, as it is derived from a pagan calendar symbol marking the winter solstice—a circle representing the sun's course, with a dot in the center representing the earth. When this was made as a cookie, the dot became a cross; and when it was later made of one strip of rolled dough, it assumed the shape of the pretzel as we know it.

DANISH ADVENT PRETZELS

[*Adventskringler*]

PASTRY:

- 2 envelopes dry yeast
- ½ cup lukewarm water
- 2 tablespoons sugar
- 2 eggs
- 1 teaspoon salt
- Grated rind of ½ lemon
- ¾ cup softened unsalted butter
- 4 to 5 cups flour

FILLING:

- 4 tablespoons butter
- 1 cup fine granulated sugar
- ¾ cup blanched, finely chopped almonds
- 1 egg white, lightly beaten

TOPPING:

- 1 well-beaten egg
- 10 to 12 sugar cubes, coarsely crushed
- ¾ cup coarsely chopped unblanched almonds, approximately

Sprinkle yeast into lukewarm water, add 1 tablespoon sugar and set aside in a warm place for 5 to 10 minutes, or until mixture foams. Beat eggs well and add to yeast mixture along with salt, lemon rind and remaining tablespoonful of sugar. Gradually work in softened butter and enough flour to make a firm but pliable dough. Knead well for 10 minutes, or until surface blisters and dough is smooth and elastic. Place in a floured bowl, dust top with flour, cover lightly and set to rise in a draft-free corner for about 25 minutes, or until puffy but not quite doubled in bulk. Punch down, knead lightly for 2 or 3 minutes and roll to a long strip, about 4½ inches wide and ¼ inch thick. This will be a very long strip that will make a huge pretzel about 24 inches in width. If you do not have a baking sheet large enough to hold this, or if you do not feel up to handling a piece of pastry this large, divide dough in half and roll in 2 strips to make two 12-inch-wide pretzels. However, the large size will have a better shape and will make a more impressive centerpiece.

To make filling, rub butter, sugar and nuts together until crumbly. Sprinkle down center of dough strip. Fold half of the dough over one third of the way. Bring the second half over to close the roll, sealing the edges with egg white. Gently flip roll over onto lightly buttered baking sheet, so seam is on bottom. Trim two ends of strip and bring them together, drawing them into the middle of the circle to form a pretzel. Do not twist or knot these strips. Seal ends to inside top of pretzel. Seal with egg white. Cover loosely and set to rise in a draft-free corner for 20 minutes.

Brush the pretzel with beaten whole egg and sprinkle with coarsely crushed sugar and nuts. Bake in preheated 425° oven for about 20 minutes, or until light golden brown.

Makes 1 large or 2 small pretzels

FINNISH VIIPURI TWIST

[*Viipurinrinkilä*]

It is believed that this was first baked by a Finnish monk in the fifteenth century.

- 2 envelopes dry yeast
- ½ cup lukewarm water
- ¾ cup sugar
- 1½ cups milk
- 4 tablespoons unsalted butter
- 1 teaspoon salt
- ½ teaspoon nutmeg
- 1 teaspoon crushed cardamom seeds
- 7 to 8 cups flour, as needed

Sprinkle yeast into lukewarm water with 1 tablespoon sugar and set aside in a warm place for 5 to 10 minutes, or until foamy. Scald milk and add remaining sugar, butter and salt. When butter has melted, remove from heat, cool to lukewarm and add nutmeg and cardamom. Combine with yeast mixture and gradually stir in enough flour to make a fairly stiff dough. Knead for about 10 minutes, or until dough is smooth and elastic and surface blisters. Place in a floured bowl, dust dough lightly with flour, cover loosely and set to rise in a draft-free corner until doubled in bulk—about 1 to 1½ hours. Punch down and knead lightly for 2 or 3 minutes, or until elastic and pliable.

Roll into a sausage shape about 4 feet long and 1½ inches in diameter at the center, tapering out toward each end. Draw ends in to form a circle; then twist them around each other twice and draw inside to form pretzel, attaching ends to make design shown. Slide onto buttered baking sheet. Cover lightly and let rise until puffy but not quite double in bulk—about 30 minutes. Sprinkle liberally with boiling water. Bake in preheated 425° oven for 45 minutes, or until golden brown. Sprinkle with boiling water two or three times during baking and again when twist is taken from the oven. This tastes best if it is allowed to remain uncut for 2 or 3 days.

Makes a 12- by 8-inch pretzel

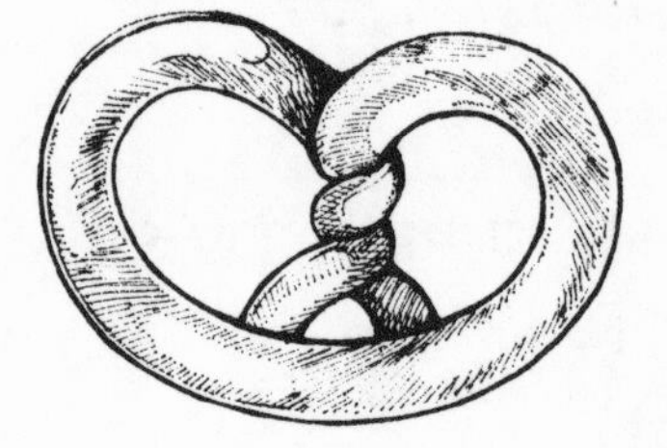

BREAD DOLLS

Many European and South American countries make dolls of sweet yeast dough to delight children at Christmas breakfasts and dinners. In Ecuador and Guatemala these carefully modeled dolls are decorated with brilliantly colored sugar icing, and in Peru bright feather headdresses are often added—a touch that makes the dolls look like something the Incas might have used to celebrate one of their own festivals. The Swiss Grittibanz vary in size from 8 inches to 2 feet and wear braids or Alpine hats and leather shorts and, like the amusing Finnish doll faces, the Pullaukkoja, are decorated only with raisins or currants to mark their eyes, noses, mouths and buttons.

2 envelopes dry yeast
½ cup lukewarm water
1 tablespoon sugar
1¼ cups milk
1 cup (½ pound) unsalted butter
1¼ cups sugar
1 teaspoon salt
2 eggs
Grated rind of 1 lemon; or 1 teaspoon vanilla; or 1½ teaspoon mixed powdered spices to taste; or 1 teaspoon crushed anise; or ½ teaspoon cardamom
6 to 7 cups flour
1 egg yolk beaten with 1 tablespoon milk
1 egg white, beaten
Raisins, currants, or Decorative Sugar Icing, page 207

Sprinkle yeast into lukewarm water, add 1 tablespoon sugar, cover loosely and set aside in a warm place for 5 to 10 minutes, or until foamy. Scald milk, add butter and stir over low heat until butter melts. Remove from heat and stir in sugar and salt. Cool to lukewarm. Add to yeast mixture with eggs, flavoring and half the flour. Mix well until free of lumps. Gradually beat in as much remaining flour as necessary to make a dough that is just smooth enough to begin to leave the sides of the bowl, but one that is still very soft and pliable.

Place dough in a clean bowl, cover loosely with waxed paper and chill in refrigerator 5 or 6 hours, or overnight. Punch dough down the first two or three times it rises. Punch dough down, knead

2 or 3 minutes and divide into portions large enough to make the size dolls you want. Shape as shown. Remember that this dough will swell, so make arms and legs thin enough. Pat or roll into shapes with your hands. Attach heads, arms, legs, etc., with milk so they will stick. Place on buttered baking sheets, cover loosely and set to rise in a draft-free corner until not quite doubled in bulk—about 30 minutes. Brush with hot water and bake in preheated 350° oven for 1 hour, or until golden brown and done. Sprinkle with hot water once or twice during baking. Five minutes before end of baking time, brush dolls with egg yolk glaze and continue baking until done. Stick raisin or currant eyes, nose, mouth and buttons on with beaten egg white while dolls are hot.

Dolls that are to be decorated with icing must first be completely cold.

Makes about eight 8-inch dolls, or 15 to 20 Finnish doll faces

Variation: The dough used for the Finnish Viipuri Twist (page 19) can also be used for dolls. If you like, raisins or currants and diced candied fruit peel can be added to either dough.

CZECHOSLOVAKIAN CHRISTMAS BRAID

[*Vanocka*]

2 envelopes dry yeast
½ cup lukewarm water
2 tablespoons sugar
¾ cup milk
⅔ cup sugar
1 teaspoon salt
½ cup (¼ pound) unsalted butter
Grated rind of ½ lemon
Pinch of mace, or 8 teaspoons crushed anise seeds
3 egg yolks
4 to 4½ cups flour
¾ cup presoaked raisins, well drained
½ cup coarsely chopped blanched almonds
1 egg yolk beaten with 1 tablespoon milk
Whole blanched almonds
Sugar, for sprinkling

Sprinkle yeast into lukewarm water and stir in 2 tablespoons sugar. Cover lightly and set aside in a warm place for 5 to 10 minutes, or until foamy. Scald milk and stir in ⅔ cup sugar, salt and butter. When butter melts, cool milk to lukewarm and add lemon rind and mace or anise. Add, with egg yolks, to yeast mixture. Gradually stir in enough flour to make a fairly stiff, smooth dough that leaves the sides of the bowl. Knead on a floured board for about 10 minutes, or until dough is smooth and elastic and blisters on the surface. Add more flour, if necessary, during kneading. Place in a floured bowl, dust top of dough with flour, cover lightly and set to rise in a draft-free corner until doubled in bulk—about 1 to 1½ hours.

Dredge drained raisins and nuts with a little flour, shaking off excess. Punch dough down and knead fruit and nuts into dough only until well distributed. Divide dough into 8 equal parts. Form each into a roll about 14 inches long. Braid 4 rolls together, starting in the middle and working out toward each end. Moisten the top of the first braid with a little milk and place second braid of 3 rolls on top, lengthwise down the center. Cut remaining roll in half lengthwise to make 2 thinner rolls. Twist these together to resemble a rope. Moisten top of second braid with a little milk and place twisted roll down the center. Tuck all braid ends under to secure them. Cover lightly and let rise again until puffy but not quite doubled—about 30 minutes.

Brush with egg yolk glaze and sprinkle with almonds. Bake in preheated 325° oven for about 1 hour, or until golden brown and hollow-sounding when tapped. Sprinkle with sugar while warm. For best flavor, do not cut for 24 hours.

Makes a large loaf about 12 inches long

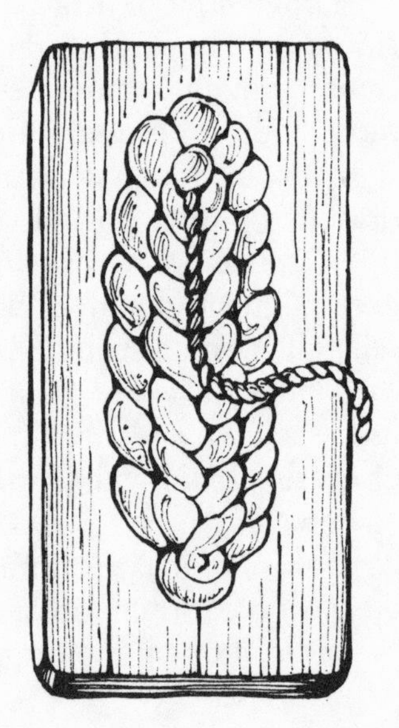

AUSTRIAN CHRISTMAS BRAID

[*Striezel*]

Follow preceding recipe, substituting 2 whole eggs plus 2 yolks for the 3 egg yolks. Do not use mace or anise. Raisins and/or nuts may be used or eliminated, to taste.

This bread is shaped of 3 braids in graduated sizes. Use 3 large rolls for the bottom braid, 3 medium-size rolls for the second braid and 3 small rolls for the top braid. Arrange and attach. After braided bread has risen, brush with the egg yolk glaze and bake, eliminating almonds. Dust with sugar while warm, or spread with Creamy Sugar Glaze, page 205, when cool.

This is also sometimes prepared more as a bread, without any raisins or nuts and with only half the amount of sugar. Braid as above; sprinkle with coarse salt and caraway seeds before baking.

DUTCH RAISIN BREAD

[*Krentenbrood*]

1 recipe Czechoslovakian Christmas Braid, page 23, substituting 1 whole egg for 3 yolks, and eliminating mace
1 cup golden raisins
¾ cup currants
½ cup rum or brandy
Flour for dredging

FILLING:

1 cup blanched almonds, finely ground
¾ cup fine granulated sugar
2 or 3 drops almond extract
1 egg white, stiffy beaten

Prepare dough and let rise until double in bulk.

Soak raisins and currants in brandy for ½ hour. Drain well and dredge lightly with flour, shaking off excess. Knead raisins and currants into dough after it has risen and has been punched down.

Prepare filling by combining ground almonds, sugar and almond extract and working in stiffly beaten egg white until mixture is dry enough to knead. Knead until smooth and workable. Divide paste in half and shape each half into a roll about 1 inch in diameter.

Divide dough in half. Flatten each half into a rectangle about 7 inches long. Place a strip of almond paste lengthwise down the center of each dough rectangle. Fold and shape dough around paste to enclose it and form a loaf. Place each loaf in well-buttered 7-inch bread-loaf pan. Cover lightly and let rise until doubled in bulk—about 1 to 1½ hours. Bake in preheated 375° oven for 45 minutes to 1 hour.

Makes 2 loaves

LITHUANIAN HONEY AND POPPY SEED BREAD

[*Kaledu Pyragas*]

1 recipe Czechoslovakian Christmas Braid, page 23, substituting 2 whole eggs for 3 yolks and eliminating mace and anise seeds
½ cup poppy seeds, approximately
2 cups golden raisins
½ cup honey, approximately

Prepare dough, adding ⅓ cup poppy seeds to the yeast mixture when you combine it with the eggs and the milk and butter mixture. When dough has risen, punch it down and knead in raisins only until they are well distributed. Divide dough in half and shape to fit two 7-inch bread-loaf pans. Place dough in buttered pans, cover lightly and let rise again until doubled in bulk—about 1 to 1½ hours. Bake in preheated 350° oven for about 1 hour, or until golden brown and hollow-sounding when tapped. Five minutes before bread is done, brush top with honey that has been slightly warmed and sprinkle with remaining poppy seeds. Bake 5 minutes longer.

Makes 2 loaves

DRESDEN STOLLEN

[*Germany—Christstollen*]

½ cup rum or brandy
1 cup chopped citron
1 cup chopped candied orange peel
¾ cup golden raisins
¾ cup currants
2 envelopes dry yeast
½ cup lukewarm water
1 cup plus 1 tablespoon sugar
2 cups milk
2 teaspoons salt
1⅓ cups unsalted butter
Grated rind of 1½ lemons
1 teaspoon almond extract
7 to 8 cups flour, as needed
4 eggs, lightly beaten
1½ cups chopped blanched almonds
½ cup melted butter, approximately
⅓ to ½ cup granulated sugar, for sprinkling
Vanilla Sugar (confectioners'), page 211, for sprinkling

Combine rum with citron, orange peel, raisins and currants and let stand for 1 hour. Drain, reserving rum and fruit. Dissolve yeast in lukewarm water, sprinkle with 1 tablespoon sugar and set aside in a warm place for 10 minutes, or until foamy. Scald milk with 1 cup granulated sugar, salt and butter. When butter melts, cool to lukewarm. Add lemon rind, 2 tablespoons reserved rum and almond extract. Stir in yeast and 2 cups flour. Mix well and set in warm corner for 30 minutes, or until the mixture bubbles. Stir in eggs and work in as much remaining flour as needed to make a soft, light dough that does not stick to your hands.

Dredge drained fruit lightly with flour. Turn dough onto floured board and knead until dough blisters and is smooth and elastic. Knead in fruits and nuts only until well distributed. Gather into a ball, place in a floured bowl and dust top lightly with flour. Cover loosely and let rise in a draft-free corner for 1 hour, or until doubled in bulk. Punch dough down, divide into thirds and set aside for 10 minutes. Lightly roll each third of dough into an oval about ¾ inch thick. Brush top of each oval with a little melted butter and sprinkle with a tablespoonful or two of granulated sugar. Fold each oval lengthwise, almost in half, so that edges do not quite meet. Press closed. Slide loaves onto a lightly buttered baking sheet, brush tops with melted butter and let rise in draft-free corner for 1 hour, or until almost doubled in bulk. Bake in preheated

375° oven for about 1 hour, or until golden brown and hollow-sounding when tapped on bottom. Cool slightly, but while still warm, brush tops with melted butter and dust with confectioners' sugar. Cool completely and dust with confectioners' sugar again before slicing. Serve thinly sliced, with or without butter. To store, place in plastic bags and tie closed, or wrap in double thickness of aluminum foil.

Makes 3 loaves

SWEDISH SAFFRON BUNS

[*Saffransbröd*]

Served on December 13th, Saint Lucia's Day, these buns are made in many shapes, each with its own name, the most popular being the Lussekatter, or Lucia Cats. Some of these are set aside after Christmas and are crumbled into the seeds for the next season's grain sowing, symbolizing the life cycle.

½ teaspoon dried saffron threads
1 cup half-and-half (milk and cream)
2 envelopes dry yeast
¼ cup lukewarm water
1 tablespoon sugar
⅓ cup sugar
1 teaspoon salt
⅓ cup unsalted butter
1 egg, beaten
4 cups sifted flour, or as needed
1 egg yolk beaten with 1 tablespoon milk
1 egg white, beaten
Raisins or currants, for decorations
Lump sugar, crushed
Grated blanched almonds

Crush dry saffron to a fine powder and steep in 1 or 2 tablespoons lukewarm half-and-half for 10 minutes. Sprinkle yeast into ¼ cup lukewarm water, add 1 tablespoon sugar, cover lightly and set aside in a warm place for 5 to 10 minutes, or until foamy. Scald remaining half-and-half and add ⅓ cup sugar, salt and butter, and stir until butter melts. Cool to lukewarm. Add to yeast mixture along with strained saffron milk (if you are sure all saffron is dissolved, straining is unnecessary) and 1 beaten egg. Mix well.

Gradually stir in flour until mixture is smooth and not sticky, but still soft and pliable. Knead for 10 minutes, or until shiny and elastic. Place in a lightly floured bowl, dust top of dough with flour, cover loosely and set to rise in draft-free corner until double in bulk —about 1½ hours. Punch dough down and knead for 2 or 3 minutes. Shape in any of the following forms, depending on the finished buns or cakes you want. Let rise 30 minutes and bake in preheated 400° oven for 10 minutes. Reduce heat to 350° and bake 30 minutes more, or until golden brown.

Makes about 2 dozen buns or 1 large or 2 small coffee cakes

Lussekatter—Lucia Cats: Pinch off small bits of dough and roll into sausage shapes 5 to 7 inches long. Place these strips together in pairs, pinching centers to join them and coiling four ends out. Brush with egg yolk glaze and bake. Using a little egg white, stick a raisin or currant in the center of each coil of the hot buns.

Julgalt—Christmas "S": Roll piece of dough to 7-inch sausage, twist into "S," brush with egg glaze, bake, then dot with raisins or currants, using a little egg white.

Gulluagn—Double "S": Form two 9-inch sausage rolls, twist each into an "S" and place one over the other, brushing under the top "S" with milk to make them stick. Brush with egg yolk glaze, bake, then dot with raisins or currants, using a little egg white.

(continued)

Praestens Har—Priests' Hair: This is a larger pastry, for which you need 3 rolls about 7 inches long. Curl each one, then insert one within the other, sealing them together with milk. Brush with egg yolk glaze, bake, then dot with raisins or currants, using a little egg white.

Luciakrona—Lucia Crown: Form seven 7-inch rolls. Then roll half of each roll flat. Coil top half of strips as for "S" buns and place them next to each other to form a tiara effect. Twine flat ends around each other to join coils. Brush with egg yolk glaze, bake, then dot with raisins, using a little egg white.

Julbrød—Saffron Braid: Shape dough into 3 ropes, then braid. Brush with egg yolk glaze and sprinkle with sugar and/or grated blanched almonds. Bake at 400° for 10 minutes, lower heat to 350° and bake about 50 minutes more, or until cake sounds hollow when tapped on bottom.

Julkaka—Christmas Cake: Shape dough into a large cake. To make the round cake, form one continuous long sausage roll of all the dough and then coil it. With a scissors, make 1-inch-deep cuts 2 inches apart around the outside roll. Brush with egg yolk glaze and sprinkle with coarsely crushed cube sugar. Raisins may be kneaded into the dough. Bake as for Julbrød (page 30).

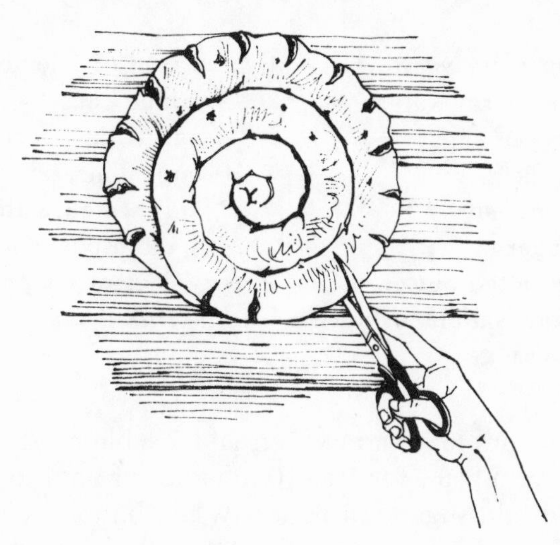

CORNISH SAFFRON BREAD

[*England*]

1 recipe Swedish Saffron Buns, page 28, made with 1 teaspoon saffron and 3 to 3½ cups flour
¾ cup mixed diced candied fruit peel
¾ cup golden raisins
¾ cup currants
¾ cup chopped walnuts or blanched almonds
1 egg yolk beaten with 1 tablespoon milk
Sugar

When dough has risen, punch it down, knead for 2 or 3 minutes, then knead in lightly floured fruits and nuts. Divide dough in half, shape into loaves and place in 2 well-buttered 7-inch loaf pans. Let rise until doubled in bulk, brush with egg glaze and sprinkle with sugar. Bake in preheated 350° oven for 1 to 1½ hours.

Makes 2 loaves

UKRAINIAN BRAIDED BREAD

[*Kolach*]

Three of these handsome bread rings are stacked upon each other, and a candle burns in the top ring to adorn the holiday table.

- 4 envelopes dry yeast
- ⅔ cup lukewarm water
- 2 tablespoons sugar
- 2 cups milk
- 1½ teaspoons salt
- 1¼ cups sugar
- 1⅓ cups unsalted butter
- 1½ teaspoons vanilla, or juice of 1 orange
- Grated rind of 1 lemon
- 5 whole eggs
- 6 egg yolks
- 9–10 cups flour, or as needed
- 1 egg beaten with 2 tablespoons milk
- Poppy seeds or chopped nuts, for sprinkling

Sprinkle yeast into lukewarm water, add 2 tablespoons sugar and set aside in warm place for 5 to 10 minutes, or until foamy. Scald milk and add salt, sugar and butter. When butter melts, remove from heat and cool to lukewarm. Stir in vanilla or orange juice and lemon rind. Beat whole eggs with yolks and add to yeast mixture along with the butter and milk. Beat thoroughly, gradually sifting in flour until you have a firm but still pliable dough. Knead for 10 minutes, or until dough is shiny and elastic and surface blisters. Place in a floured bowl, dust top of dough with flour, cover loosely and set to rise in a draft-free corner until doubled in bulk—about 1 to 1½ hours.

Punch down and let rise again until doubled. Punch down and divide dough in thirds. Knead each third for 2 or 3 minutes and form as follows. Divide each piece of dough into 3 equal parts. Roll each of these pieces into a long sausage shape about 1½ inches in diameter. Braid these together, working from the middle out toward each end. Turn ends together to form rings. Place each ring in a well-buttered 10-inch tube pan.

Cover loosely and set to rise in draft-free corner until almost doubled in bulk. Brush with egg glaze, sprinkle with poppy seeds or nuts and bake in preheated 375° oven for 10 minutes. Lower heat to 325° and continue baking for about 1 hour, or until golden brown and hollow-sounding when tapped. Cool in pan for 10 minutes and turn onto a rack.

Makes 3 rings

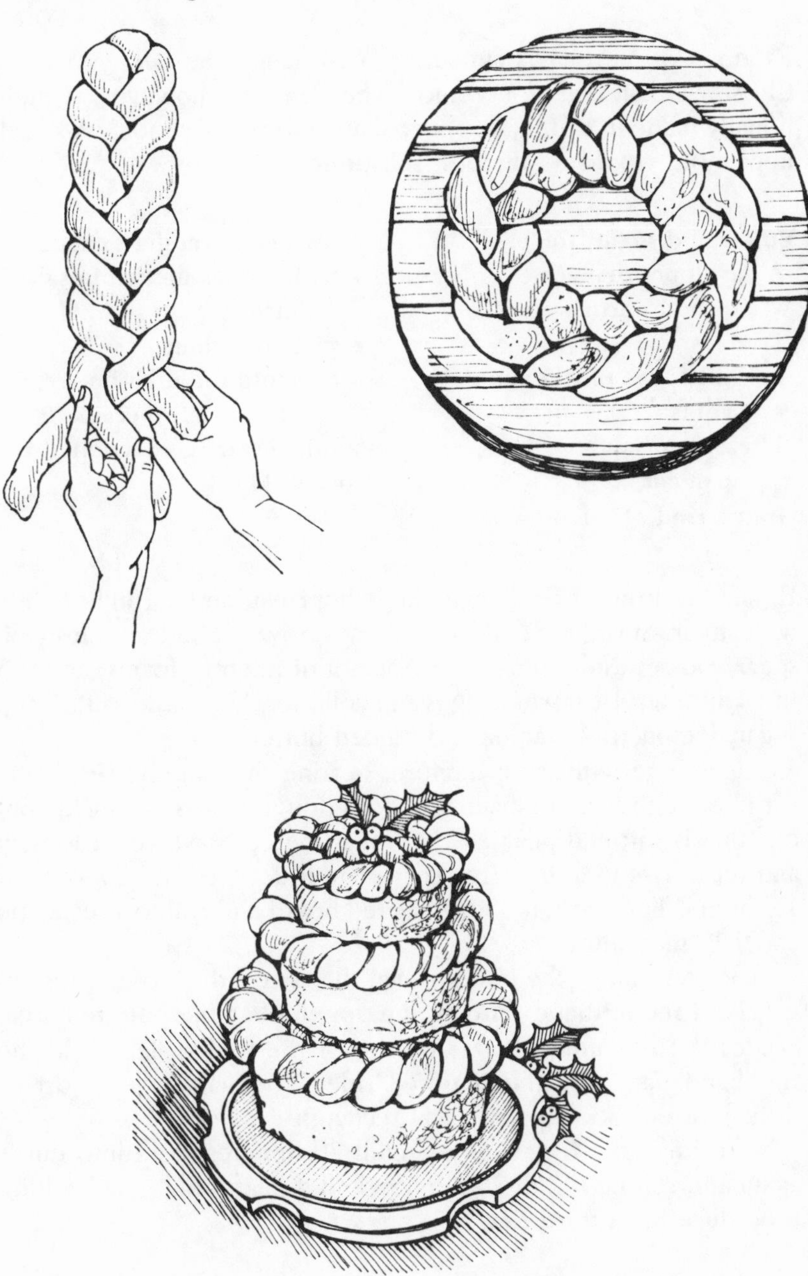

GOLDEN BREAD OF VERONA

[*Italy*]

Pandoro di Verona is similar to Veneziana, the yeasty, buttery Christmas coffeecake of Venice. The Pandoro, however, is traditionally made in a high, thin, star-shaped tower of a mold. A kugelhopf mold would be the best substitute.

Butter and sugar, for pan
2 envelopes dry yeast
¼ cup lukewarm water
1 tablespoon sugar
2 whole eggs plus 3 egg yolks
1 teaspoon salt
⅓ cup sugar
Grated rind of 1 lemon
2 teaspoons vanilla extract
4 tablespoons melted unsalted butter
2 to 3 cups flour
⅔ cup cold unsalted butter, cut in small pieces
Vanilla Sugar (confectioner's; page 211)

Butter the inside of a 2-quart kugelhopf pan and sprinkle lightly with sugar. Sprinkle yeast into lukewarm water, add 1 tablespoon sugar and set aside in a warm place until mixture foams, about 5 to 10 minutes. Beat whole eggs and yolks together. Add salt, ⅓ cup sugar, lemon rind, vanilla and melted butter.

Combine with yeast mixture, beating thoroughly. Gradually stir in enough flour to make a smooth dough that is not sticky, but one that is soft and pliable. Place in a floured bowl, cover loosely and set to rise in a draft-free corner until doubled in bulk—about 1½ hours. Turn dough onto a floured board and roll to a rectangle about ½ inch thick.

Scatter half of the butter down the center third of the rectangle. Fold the lefthand third of the dough over the buttered area. Scatter the remaining butter on top of the folded flap. Fold the righthand flap over the buttered side. You will have a sort of three-layered, booklike, vertical rectangle.

Roll flat in a rectangle and chill 20 minutes. Fold into thirds again and roll flat. Chill 20 minutes and repeat folding and rolling procedure for a third time.

After the third rolling, chill 10 minutes. Then roll the dough lengthwise, jelly-roll fashion. Place in a ring in the prepared kugelhopf pan. Cover loosely and let rise for about 1 hour and 15 minutes, or until doubled in bulk. Preheat oven to 400°F. Bake for 10 minutes, then reduce heat to 350° and bake 30 to 40 minutes more, or until a tester comes out clean. Cool on a rack, then dust with vanilla sugar.

Makes 1 loaf

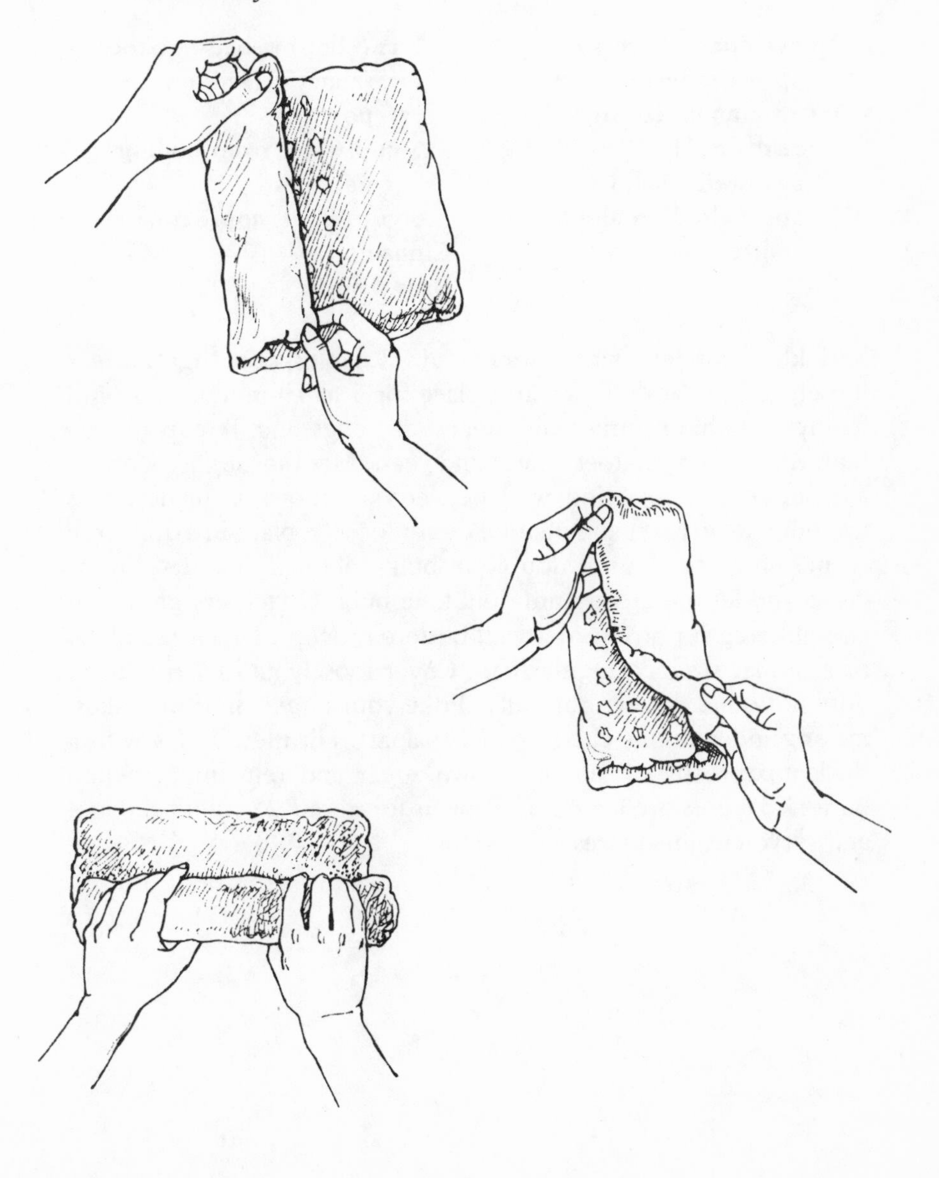

MORAVIAN SUGAR CAKE

This cake and the buns that follow are served by the Moravians in Pennsylvania and parts of the South for their Christmas and New Year celebrations, two of the five "love feasts" they hold during the year to commemorate the Last Supper, a custom handed down from early Christian times.

- **2 envelopes dry yeast**
- **½ cup warm water**
- **1 cup granulated sugar**
- **1 teaspoon salt**
- **2 eggs, well beaten**
- **1¼ cups melted unsalted butter**
- **1 cup hot mashed potatoes (about 2 medium potatoes)**
- **½ cup water from boiling potatoes**
- **4 cups flour, approximately**
- **Cinnamon**
- **Brown sugar**

Sprinkle yeast into warm water, add 1 tablespoon sugar, cover loosely and set aside in a warm place for 5 to 10 minutes, or until foamy. Combine remaining sugar, salt, eggs and ¾ cup melted butter. Add hot potatoes, water and yeast. Mix thoroughly. Gradually sift in flour, stirring well between additions, until dough is smooth but very soft and pliable. Cover loosely, place in a draft-free corner and let rise until double in bulk—about 1½ hours. Punch down and let rise again until double in bulk. Divide dough in half and place each portion in a well-buttered, deep 11-inch pie plate, or a similar size rectangular pan. Cover loosely and let rise again until not quite double but puffy. Poke your fingers into the cakes, making indentations about 2 inches apart. Fill these holes with a thick mixture of cinnamon, brown sugar and remaining melted butter. Bake in preheated 350° oven for about 25 minutes. Cool and serve cut in squares or wedges.

Makes 2 cakes

MORAVIAN LOVE FEAST BUNS

Prepare dough as in preceding recipe. After it has risen for the second time, punch it down and knead until smooth. Pinch off pieces and shape into balls about 3 inches in diameter. Place 4 inches apart on a buttered baking sheet, cover loosely and let rise again until not quite double in bulk. Bake in preheated 375° oven for about 30 minutes. Brush with a little melted butter as buns begin to brown. Cool and serve.

Makes about a dozen buns

WIGS

[*England*]

These caraway buns float in the wassail bowls of Shropshire, instead of the usual toast. They are also good served warm from the oven and freshly buttered to accompany coffee on Christmas morning.

4 envelopes dry yeast
¾ cup lukewarm water
1 tablespoon sugar
1½ cups half-and-half (milk and cream)
½ cup (¼ pound) unsalted butter
½ cup sugar
2 teaspoons salt
1 teaspoon nutmeg
Pinch each of mace and cloves
1 tablespoon caraway seeds lightly crushed
7 to 8 cups flour, or as needed
1 egg, well beaten

Sprinkle yeast into lukewarm water, add 1 tablespoon sugar and set aside in a warm place for 5 to 10 minutes, or until foamy. Scald half-and-half and add butter, stirring until it melts. Remove from heat and add remaining sugar, salt, spices and caraway seeds; cool to lukewarm. Combine with yeast mixture and gradually stir in flour until dough is smooth and not sticky but still soft and pliable. Knead for 10 minutes or until shiny and elastic. Place dough in a floured bowl, dust top with flour, cover loosely and set to rise in a draft-free corner until double in bulk—about 1 to 1½ hours. Punch dough down, knead for 2 or 3 minutes and let dough rest for 5 to 10 minutes. Divide dough into 6 pieces and shape these into large round slightly flat buns.

Place 4 inches apart on a well-buttered baking sheet and cut a deep cross into the top of each bun so that it can later be divided into triangular quarters. Cover loosely and set to rise until double in bulk—30 to 45 minutes. Brush with beaten egg and bake in preheated 400° oven for 10 minutes. Reduce heat to 350° and bake 15 minutes longer, or until golden brown and hollow-sounding when tapped.

Makes 6 buns

BREMEN KLABEN

[*Germany*]

1½ cups golden raisins
⅔ cup currants
¾ cup sliced or chopped blanched almonds
¾ cup mixed diced candied fruits
½ cup brandy
4 envelopes dry yeast
¾ cup lukewarm water
2 tablespoons sugar
¾ cup milk
½ cup (¼ pound) unsalted butter
½ cup lard
⅔ cup sugar
1 teaspoon salt
1 teaspoon rose water
½ teaspoon powdered cardamom
1 teaspoon cinnamon
Grated rind of 1 lemon and 1 orange
5 to 6 cups flour, approximately
1 egg yolk beaten with 1 tablespoon water
Blanched whole almonds

Combine raisins, currants, almonds and candied fruits and sprinkle with brandy. Let stand 1 hour, then drain, reserving fruit and brandy. Lightly dredge fruits and nuts with a little flour. Sprinkle yeast into lukewarm water, add 2 tablespoons sugar, cover lightly and set in a warm place for about 10 minutes, or until mixture foams. Meanwhile, scald milk with butter, lard, ⅔ cup sugar and salt. When fats have melted, remove milk from heat and stir in rose water, 2 teaspoons reserved brandy, spices and fruit rind. Cool to lukewarm and combine with yeast mixture in a large bowl. Sift flour in gradually, blending as you do so, until mixture is smooth enough to be kneaded. This will require about 5 cups of flour. Turn onto a floured board and knead for about 10 minutes, adding more flour as needed.

When dough is smooth and elastic and surface is blistered, gather it into a ball and place in clean, lightly floured bowl. Dust top of dough with flour, cover lightly with a kitchen towel and set to rise in a draft-free corner for 45 minutes to 1 hour, or until doubled in bulk and no longer springy when you press it down with your fingertip. Punch dough down and lightly knead in fruits and nuts. Divide in half and shape each half into a loaf, or roll into an oval and fold as for Dresden Stollen, page 27. Place on buttered baking sheet, brush with egg yolk glaze and dot with almonds. Cover lightly and set to rise in a draft-free corner for about 45 minutes, or until doubled in bulk. Bake in preheated 350° oven for about 1 hour, or until golden brown and hollow-sounding when tapped. Cool thoroughly before slicing.

Makes 2 large loaves

Variation: Since it is made without eggs, the above version results in a breadlike loaf. If you would like a slightly richer, more cakelike result, beat 2 eggs lightly and add them to the yeast mixture along with the milk.

DURHAM CURRANT BREAD

[*England*]

Following preceding recipe. Flavor with ½ teaspoon each cinnamon, nutmeg and allspice and ¼ teaspoon powdered cloves. Knead 1 cup of currants and 1 cup golden raisins into dough after it has risen. Divide dough in half and place each half in a buttered 7-inch loaf pan. Let rise until double in bulk, and bake.

SCANDINAVIAN CARDAMOM BREAD

[*Norway, Denmark, Sweden, Finland, Iceland*]

Prepare dough as for Bremen Klaben, page 38, with the following changes. Use 2 teaspoons powdered cardamom and omit cinnamon. Use 1 cup unsalted butter and omit lard. Use only raisins and candied fruit peels and omit currants and nuts. Use only ½ cup sugar. When dough has risen, it may be shaped into 1 large or 2 small rounds or loaves, or divide it into thirds, shape into 3 sausage rolls and braid together. Place on a buttered baking sheet or in a loaf pan or a long, narrow 8-inch coffee-cake pan. After shaping, let rise until almost double in bulk, and bake.

DANISH CHRISTMAS CAKE

[*Julekage*]

Prepare dough as for Bremen Klaben, page 38, but use an extra ½ cup butter and no lard. When dough has risen, punch it down and roll out to a rectangle about ¼ to ½ inch thick. Dot this with remaining ½ cup cold butter cut into small pieces. Fold dough in overlapping thirds and roll out again (see illustration on page 35). Chill 20 minutes, fold in thirds and roll again. Chill 20 minutes and repeat folding and rolling. Place in buttered 9-inch spring form, cover loosely and let rise until doubled in bulk. Brush with beaten whole egg and pour over cake 3 tablespoons melted butter. Sprinkle with coarsely crushed cubed sugar and halved blanched almonds. Bake in preheated 400° oven for 10 minutes, reduce heat to 350° and continue baking for 45 minutes. If you like, some cinnamon, sugar, raisins and/or finely minced candied fruit peel can be sprinkled over rectangle of dough before the third folding and rolling.

BASIC COFFEECAKE DOUGH

3 envelopes dry yeast
½ cup lukewarm water
⅓ to ½ cup sugar
¾ cup milk
½ cup (¼ pound) unsalted butter
1 teaspoon salt
Grated rind of 1 lemon
Flavoring as called for
5 cups flour, approximately
4 egg yolks and 1 whole egg, or 3 whole eggs

Sprinkle yeast into lukewarm water, add 2 tablespoons sugar and set aside in a draft-free corner for 5 to 10 minutes or until mixture foams. Scald milk and to it add butter, remaining sugar and salt. Stir until butter melts. Cool until lukewarm and add lemon rind and flavoring. Combine 2 cups flour, yeast, eggs and milk mixture and beat thoroughly. Gradually add enough remaining flour to make a smooth but pliable dough. Turn out on a floured board and knead for about 10 minutes, adding flour if needed, until dough is smooth and elastic and blisters form on the surface.

Gather dough into a ball, place in a floured bowl, dust top with flour and cover lightly with a towel. Set to rise in a draft-free corner until doubled in bulk—about 1 to 1½ hours. Punch dough down, knead for 2 or 3 minutes. Add other ingredients and shape as called for in individual recipes. Let rise until doubled in bulk after shaping and bake as directed.

Makes 2 large coffeecakes or 1 huge braided loaf

Rich Coffeecake Dough: Prepare as in preceding recipe, using 10 egg yolks, 1 cup butter and ½ cup milk instead of the amounts called for.

POPPY SEED HORSESHOE

[*Hungary—Makos Patko*]

This is the highlight of the Christmas sweet table in Hungary. The Polish Strucla z Makiem, the Ukrainian Makivnyk, the Yugoslavian Potica and the Putiza of the Veneto region of Italy are made exactly the same way.

FILLING:

¾ pound poppy seeds
½ cup (¼ pound) unsalted butter
½ cup honey
3 tablespoons light sweet cream
½ cup chopped raisins
Grated rind of 1 lemon or ½ orange
½ teaspoon cinnamon, or to taste
Optional additions: 1 grated sour apple or 2 tablespoons apple butter, ½ cup chopped walnuts

PASTRY:

1 recipe Basic Coffeecake Dough, page 41, made with 2 whole eggs and 2 yolks
White Sugar Glaze, page 206, or 1 egg beaten with 1 tablespoon water

The night before you intend to make this cake, cover poppy seeds with boiling water and let them soak until the following morning, or wash and parboil for 30 minutes just before grinding. Drain thoroughly and grind in a poppy-seed grinder, or put them through the finest blade of your meat chopper 3 or 4 times, or until they are very finely pulverized. (Or buy ground poppy seeds if there is a store near you that prepares them, but be sure they are not rancid.)

Cream butter with honey. When well blended, combine with cream, poppy seeds and remaining filling ingredients. (Some people prefer to omit the butter and to cook the ground poppy seeds with 2 cups milk and the honey until the mixture is thick. The other ingredients are then stirred in.)

Prepare dough, and when it has risen, punch down and roll out to a rectangle a little less than ¼ inch thick. Spread filling over dough and roll up jelly-roll fashion. Bend roll gently into a horseshoe shape and slide onto a buttered baking sheet. Or cut in half and place each half in a buttered 9-inch loaf pan or on a baking sheet. Let rise until almost doubled in bulk.

If you want to ice the roll, brush it with lukewarm water before baking. Otherwise, brush it with egg glaze. Bake in preheated 350° oven for about 45 minutes, or until golden brown. Cool thoroughly before icing.

Makes 1 large or 2 smaller coffeecakes

NUT ROLL

[*Eastern Europe*]

FILLING:

3 eggs
½ cup sugar
2 cups grated walnuts, almonds or hazelnuts
½ cup (¼ pound) melted unsalted butter
Grated rind of 3 lemons or 2 oranges
½ teaspoon cinnamon or 1 teaspoon vanilla extract

PASTRY:

1 recipe Basic Coffeecake Dough, page 41, made with 2 whole eggs and 2 yolks

Beat eggs with sugar until mixture is thick and pale yellow. Stir in nuts and remaining ingredients. This mixture can also be prepared by beating egg yolks with sugar, stirring in nuts and remaining ingredients, then folding in stiffly beaten whites. Prepare dough, fill roll and bake, as in preceding recipe.

Variation: In Yugoslavia 3 ounces (squares) of grated bitter chocolate are added to the nut mixture.

ITALIAN PANETTONE

[*Panettone di Milano*]

It is said that this round, high-crowned bread was created by a Milan baker, Antonio, who improved upon a traditional Milan sweet bread, Pan di Cherubini, or Cherubs' Bread, in the hope of winning the hand of the girl he loved. It became known as "Tony's Bread"—"Pane de Toni"—and is featured at Christmas; it is also baked at Easter, when it is made in the shape of a dove and is called Colombo di Pasqua.

1 recipe Rich Coffeecake Dough, page 41, using only 8 egg yolks and adding 1 tablespoon grated lemon rind and an extra ¼ cup sugar
1 cup golden and black raisins combined
½ cup minced citron
Melted butter

Prepare dough, using substitutions and additions. When dough has risen, punch down and knead in lightly floured raisins and citron, kneading only until fruit is well distributed. There are several ways to achieve the high round shape characteristic of this bread. The easiest is to place the dough in 2 medium-sized or 1 large Russian Kulich mold, which has been buttered and lined with buttered brown paper. Fill only halfway, let dough rise until doubled in bulk and then bake. If you cannot get these high cylindrical molds, divide dough in half, shape into large round loaves, place on a buttered baking sheet, cut a cross on the top of each and encircle each with a 5- or 6-inch-high tube of buttered stiff brown paper, which should then be tied firmly in place. Or place each half of the dough in an 8-inch round deep cake pan or a straight-sided 2 quart Dutch oven, well buttered, and cut a cross in the top of each. After shaping, let dough rise until almost double in bulk. Brush with melted butter and place in preheated 400° oven for 10 to 12 minutes. Place a small piece of butter in the center of the cross, reduce heat to 350° and bake for about 45 minutes, or until golden brown. The crown serves as a cover once the Panettone has been cut. Cut crown off as a top slice, then cut bread, as needed, in round crosswise slices which can then be halved or quartered. After each serving, replace crown and keep cake in an airtight plastic bag. Stored this way, it will keep for several weeks.

Makes 1 large or 2 smaller loaves

Note: Panettone may be served sprinkled with confectioners' sugar, buttered or plain. It is also excellent toasted, and it is traditional to toast the bottom slice and the crown when the rest of it has been eaten.

SOUTH AMERICAN PAN DULCE or PAN DE FIESTA and GENOESE PAN DOLCE

These three are made in a rounder shape than the Panettone, or are sometimes baked in loaf pans. They usually include candied orange peel and angelica, as well as citron. The round Pan Dolce of Friuli is flavored with nutmeg and mace or cinnamon and is made with minced citron, raisins and coarsely chopped candied cherries.

ENGLISH BOXING DAY CAKE

Prepare Basic Coffeecake Dough, page 41, adding 1 teaspoon cinnamon, ¼ teaspoon each cloves and nutmeg to the yeast with the eggs. Add only 1 tablespoon sugar to yeast. After dough has risen, punch down and knead in ¼ cup light brown sugar along with ¾ cup currants, ½ cup raisins and ¼ cup mixed diced candied fruit peel. Place in 2 deep 8-inch round buttered cake pans, let rise until doubled in bulk. Bake in preheated 400° oven 10 minutes. Lower heat to 350° and continue baking for 1 to 1½ hours. Brush with milk and sprinkle with sugar 5 minutes before cake is removed from oven. Serve sliced and buttered.

Makes 2 loaves

THREE KINGS' BREAD

[*Germany—Dreikönigsbröt; Denmark—Dreikonigebrød*]

Prepare Basic Coffeecake Dough, page 41, flavoring it with 1 teaspoon vanilla. After it has risen, punch it down and shape into 2 round loaves—or 1 large one—each with an almond hidden in it. Place on buttered baking sheet and let rise until almost doubled in bulk. Brush top with melted butter and sprinkle with 2 teaspoons cinnamon, ¾ cup coarsely crumbled cube sugar and chopped almonds, walnuts or hazelnuts. Bake in preheated 400° oven for 10 minutes, reduce heat to 350° and continue baking for about 1 hour. The hidden almond is a promise of good luck.

Makes 1 large loaf or 2 smaller loaves

MEXICAN KINGS' CAKE

[*Rosca de Reyes*]

The person who gets the bean or china doll (representing the Christ Child) gives a party for all assembled on Candlemas Day, February 2nd. I have been told by Fred Rufe, who did so much Latin American research for La Fonda del Sol in New York, that the person who gets the bean or doll often swallows it so that he does not have to bear the expense of the next party.

Prepare Basic Coffeecake Dough, page 41. When dough has risen, punch down and knead in 2 cups lightly floured mixed candied fruits and chopped blanched almonds. Roll dough into a sausage shape. Bring ends together to form a ring. Tuck a tiny china doll or a dried lima bean into the ring and pinch dough close around it. Place on buttered baking sheet. Let rise until almost doubled in bulk. Bake in preheated 350° oven for about 1 hour, or until golden brown and hollow-sounding when tapped. Brush with milk and sprinkle with sugar for the last 5 minutes of baking.

Makes 1 cake

DUTCH THREE KINGS' BREAD

[*Dreikoningenenbrood*]

Prepare as in above recipe, eliminating candied fruits and nuts and hiding 1 whole blanched almond in the ring, as a promise of good fortune.

PORTUGUESE KINGS' CAKE

[*Bolo Rei*]

This is made and shaped like the Mexican cake on page 46, but raisins are kneaded into the dough along with the candied fruits and chopped almonds. Use about 2 cups combined raisins, candied peel and nuts. After shaped ring rises, brush top with beaten egg yolk and decorate with additional candied fruit, almonds and pine nuts.

GREEK HONEY NUT BREAD

[*Christopsomo*]

Prepare 1 recipe Basic Coffeecake Dough, page 41, using 3 whole eggs and 5 to 6 cups flour. Flavor with 1 teaspoon crushed mahlepi, a spice sometimes available in Greek or Middle Eastern grocery stores. If it is not, substitute 1 tablespoon crushed anise seeds. After dough has risen, punch down and knead in ⅔ cup golden raisins, ⅔ cup chopped dried soft figs and ⅔ cup chopped walnuts. Divide dough in half and place each portion in a buttered and floured 9-inch round cake pan. (If you prefer, this dough can be done in 1 large or 2 small braided loaves.) Set aside to rise until doubled in bulk.

Meanwhile, prepare a glaze by boiling for 10 minutes ⅓ cup honey with ⅓ cup white corn syrup and ¼ cup orange juice. Brush over risen loaves and top with blanched almond halves. Bake in preheated 400° oven for 10 minutes; reduce heat to 350° and continue baking for 45 minutes to 1 hour, or until golden brown and hollow-sounding when tapped. If top browns too quickly, cover with buttered brown paper. Serve sliced, with honey.

Makes 1 large or 2 smaller loaves

GREEK NEW YEAR'S BREAD

[*Vasilopita*]

St. Basil (Vassily, in Greek) is the patron saint of the Greek New Year, and this cake honoring him is served exactly on the stroke of midnight, New Year's Eve. Like so many holiday cakes, it contains a lucky coin in one portion. The first piece cut is set aside for the Holy Mother or St. Basil, and the father of the house then cuts portions for each member of the family in order of age. Leftovers are given to the poor on the following day.

Prepare 1 recipe Basic Coffeecake Dough, page 41, using only ⅓ cup butter, ⅓ cup sugar and 3 whole eggs. Work 5 to 6 cups of flour into mixture so that it is firm but still pliable. Add 2 teaspoons crushed mahlepi, a spice sometimes available in Greek or Middle Eastern grocery stores. Otherwise, substitute 1 teaspoon powdered anise and/or 1 teaspoon cinnamon. To shape, pat about three quarters of the dough into a round loaf about 1½ inches thick. Wrap silver coin in foil and insert into cake; close dough around it. Place in a buttered 10-inch spring form.

Roll most of the remaining dough into a sausage, twist it like a rope and form a circle on top of the bread. A few extra scraps of dough can be used to form the numbers of the new year. Let rise until doubled in bulk. Brush lightly with egg yolk glaze, sprinkle with sesame seeds, if you wish, and bake in preheated 400° oven for 15 minutes. Reduce heat to 350° and bake 45 minutes more.

Makes 1 large loaf

FRENCH TWELFTH NIGHT CAKE

[*Gâteau des Rois*]

After the French Revolution, when even the slightest reference to royalty was anathema to the populace, these cakes were called Gâteaux d'Égalité, Cakes of Equality.

1 envelope dry yeast
1 tablespoon lukewarm water
3 whole eggs
1 egg yolk
1 teaspoon salt
⅔ cup sugar
Grated rind of 1 lemon
Grated rind of ½ orange
1 tablespoon orange-flower water
2 cups flour
½ cup (¼ pound) softened unsalted butter, cut into small pieces
White Sugar Glaze, page 206
Candied cherries and fruit peels

Dissolve yeast to a paste in water. Beat eggs with yolk and add salt, sugar, grated rinds and orange-flower water. Combine with yeast, flour and butter and mix all ingredients with a wooden spoon until thoroughly blended and no butter shows. Chill 4 to 5 hours. Turn dough into a well-buttered 8-inch square cake pan, cover loosely and set to rise in a draft-free corner until doubled in bulk—about 3½ hours. Bake in preheated 350° oven for about 35 to 40 minutes, or until golden brown and a tester comes out clean. Cool in pan until cake shrinks away from sides. Then cool cake on a rack, spread with glaze and decorate with candied fruits.

Makes 1 cake

GALETTE DES ROIS

See page 214.

CAKES, PIES & TARTS

Chapter Two

Although there are literally dozens and dozens of good recipes for fruit cakes, each supposedly unique and original, they all fall into three categories—white, light and dark. Fruits, spices and liquors vary from one cook to another. Fruit cakes are basically English in origin, and the colonies and former colonies all include them in their holiday celebrations, varying them with local products. I have tried to include samples of each type with any important geographical variation. All of these cakes can be stored for many months. Wrap in a rum- or brandy-soaked cloth and place in an airtight container or wrap in foil and then place in the container. Or spread with Almond Paste Icing, page 206, and then with Royal Icing, page 207, and wrap in foil and place in an airtight container. All of these cakes improve with age.

SWEDISH APRICOT NUT BREAD

[*Aprikosnötbröd*]

The recipe for this golden fruit cake was given to me by Everett Holland. It is a family Christmas recipe handed down to him from his great-grandmother, who lived in northern Sweden, close to the Norwegian border.

1 cup dried apricots
½ to 1 cup brandy, as needed
1 cup sugar
2 tablespoons softened unsalted butter
1 egg, lightly beaten
Grated rind of 1 lemon
½ cup strained orange juice
2 cups flour
2½ teaspoons baking powder
½ teaspoon baking soda
½ teaspoon salt
¾ cup chopped walnuts

Soak apricots in brandy to cover for 2 to 3 hours. Drain, cut each apricot half into 6 small pieces and reserve ¼ cup brandy in which they soaked. Cream sugar and butter until light and fluffy. Add egg and lemon rind and beat until mixture is smooth and well blended. Add reserved ¼ cup brandy and orange juice. Sift flour with baking powder, soda and salt. Resift into batter gradually, stirring well between additions. Fold in nuts and cut-up apricots. Butter an 8-inch loaf pan, line with buttered brown paper and pour in batter. Let stand 20 minutes. Bake in preheated 350° oven 1 hour, or until top is golden brown and a tester comes out clean. Turn out of pan while hot, peel off paper and cool on a rack. Let mellow for 24 hours before cutting.

Makes 1 loaf cake

Variation: It may not be an authentic Swedish Christmas touch, but this cake is very good too if 1 cup tightly packed light brown sugar is used instead of the granulated sugar.

DUBLIN FRUIT CAKE

A recipe given to me by Una Healey, who brought it with her from Ireland.

- ½ cup candied cherry halves
- ¾ cup whole blanched almonds
- 1½ cups seedless black raisins
- 1½ cups golden raisins
- 1½ cups currants
- ¾ cup diced mixed candied fruit peel
- 2 tablespoons chopped peeled apple
- 2⅔ cups flour, approximately
- ½ teaspoon baking powder
- ¼ teaspoon cinnamon
- ¼ teaspoon nutmeg
- 1 cup (½ pound) unsalted butter
- 1 cup sugar
- 6 eggs
- Grated rind of ½ lemon
- ½ teaspoon vanilla extract
- ¼ teaspoon almond extract
- 3 ounces Irish whiskey
- Almond Paste Icing, page 206, and Royal Icing, page 207

Wash cherries and let them dry uncovered overnight. Grind half of the almonds and shred or coarsely chop the remaining half. Wash and dry raisins and currants. Combine all fruits and nuts and toss to mix thoroughly. Sift flour twice with baking powder and spices and set aside. Cream butter with sugar until light and fluffy. Beat eggs with lemon rind, vanilla and almond extract and add gradually to the butter mixture, beating well between additions. Sift flour in gradually, stirring with a metal spoon. Add fruits and half of the whiskey and beat until well blended.

This should be baked in an unfluted 9-inch tube pan or in a 9-inch round cake pan that is about 3 inches deep. Butter the pan and line with buttered brown paper or several thicknesses of buttered waxed paper. Turn batter into pan. If you are not using a tube pan, make a hollow in the center of the batter so it will rise evenly and be flat.

Bake in preheated 300° oven for about 4 hours, or until a tester comes out clean. If cake begins to brown too rapidly, cover with a sheet of buttered brown paper. Sprinkle with remaining whiskey as soon as you take cake from the oven. Cool in pan for 1 hour.

Invert onto rack, remove paper and cool completely. When dry, spread with Almond Paste Icing and then with Royal Icing. Store in airtight container.

Makes 1 nine-inch cake

DANISH BEER FRUIT CAKE

[*Ølfrugtbrød*]

Follow above recipe, eliminating apple, vanilla, almond extract and whiskey. Substitute ½ cup chopped figs for cherries and 1¼ cups brown sugar for white. Use only 2 eggs. Stir in ½ cup dark beer with fruits and bake in a buttered and floured 9-inch loaf pan. Spread with White Sugar Glaze, page 206.

VICTORIAN PLUM CAKE

[*England*]

- ½ pound golden raisins
- ½ pound seedless black raisins
- 1 pound currants
- ½ cup shredded blanched almonds
- ⅔ cup coarsely chopped candied cherries
- ¾ cup mixed diced candied fruit peel
- 2 cups flour
- ¼ teaspoon each allspice, cinnamon, nutmeg, ginger and powdered cloves
- 1 cup (½ pound) unsalted butter
- 1 cup firmly packed brown sugar
- 1 tablespoon golden molasses
- Grated rind of 1 orange
- Grated rind of 1 lemon
- 5 eggs
- ½ cup brandy, rum, sherry or Madeira
- Almond Paste Icing, page 206, and Royal Icing, page 207

Combine all fruits and nuts and dredge lightly with 2 or 3 tablespoons flour. Sift remaining flour with spices. Cream butter with sugar until light and fluffy. Add molasses, grated rind and eggs, one at a time, beating well between additions. Resift flour and spices into mixture and add fruit. Mix well; then stir in brandy, rum or wine, adding enough to make a soft batter that can be dropped from a spoon.

Select an 8- or 9-inch round pan that is 3 or 4 inches deep. Butter the pan, line the bottom with buttered brown paper and on top of that place a double lining of stiff greaseproof baker's paper that comes 2 inches above the sides of the pan. Pour in batter and tie a collar of stiff buttered brown paper around the outside of the pan, coming up 2 inches above the rim. Make a hollow in the center of the cake to ensure even rising and a flat top. Bake in preheated 325° oven for 1½ hours, reduce heat to 275° and bake for 3 hours longer, or until a tester comes out clean. Let cake get cold in pan, turn out, remove paper and sprinkle with more brandy, rum or wine. Store in an airtight container for two weeks before icing.

Makes 1 large cake

ENGLISH TWELFTH CAKE

This Three Kings' cake hides both a dried green pea and a bean. The bean determines the king of the evening's revelries and the pea determines the queen. Just how one can be sure that the right prize goes to the right sex is beyond me, but maybe that's part of the fun.

¼ cup white rum
½ cup golden raisins
½ cup currants
3 tablespoons diced citron
2 tablespoons diced angelica
3 tablespoons diced candied orange peel
1 cup (½ pound) unsalted butter
¾ cup sugar
4 eggs
2 tablespoons milk
½ teaspoon almond extract
3 to 3½ cups flour
1 teaspoon cinnamon
½ teaspoon nutmeg or mace
½ teaspoon allspice
½ cup slivered blanched almonds
Grated rind of 1 lemon
1 dried pea
1 dried bean
Golden Almond Icing, page 208

Combine rum with raisins, currants and candied fruits and soak for 1 hour. Drain and reserve fruit and rum. Cream butter with sugar until light and fluffy. Add eggs, one at a time, beating well between additions. Beat in milk and 2 tablespoons reserved rum and the almond extract. Dredge fruits lightly with a little flour and shake off excess. Resift remaining flour with spices and beat into batter. Add fruits, nuts and grated lemon rind, the pea and the bean, and fold in until well distributed.

Turn the batter into a 9-inch round cake pan or loaf pan that has been buttered and lined with buttered brown paper. Bake in preheated 275° oven for about 2 hours, or until a tester comes out clean. Cool cake until it shrinks from sides of pan. Turn out onto a rack, remove paper, cool cake completely and spread with icing. Let stand several hours or overnight until icing hardens.

Makes 1 cake

DUNDEE FRUIT CAKE

[*Scotland*]

¾ cup each black raisins, golden raisins and currants
¾ cup chopped or shredded mixed candied fruit peel
2¼ cups sifted flour
½ teaspoon cinnamon
¼ teaspoon nutmeg
1 cup (½ pound) unsalted butter
1¼ cups sugar
6 eggs
½ cup ground blanched almonds
Grated rind of 1 orange and 1 lemon
½ cup slivered blanched almonds

Dredge raisins, currants and fruit peel in ¼ cup flour and shake off excess. Sift remaining flour with spices. Cream butter and sugar until mixture is light and fluffy. Add eggs one at a time, beating well between additions. Sift in flour gradually, stirring well between additions. Fold in ground almonds, floured fruits and rind. Turn batter into an 8- or 9-inch round or square cake pan that is buttered and lined with buttered brown paper. Smooth top and sprinkle with slivered almonds. Bake in preheated 350° oven 1½ hours, or until cake shrinks from sides of pan. Turn out of pan and peel off paper. Cool on rack.

Makes 1 eight- or nine-inch cake

(Although it is done more for weddings than at Christmas, this cake can be covered with Almond Paste Icing, page 206, and then with Royal Icing, page 207.)

Variation: If you like your cakes on the light side, sift ½ teaspoon baking powder with the flour and use only 4 eggs.

CHERRY WHISKEY CAKE

[Scotland]

½ cup granulated sugar
½ cup light brown sugar, firmly packed
1 cup (½ pound) unsalted butter
4 eggs
¼ teaspoon nutmeg
Grated rind of 1 lemon
3 tablespoons Scotch whiskey
2 cups sifted flour
Pinch of salt
1 cup cut-up candied red cherries
2 cups currants
¾ cup mixed diced angelica, citron and candied orange peel

Combine sugars and cream with butter until light and fluffy. Add eggs, one at a time, beating well between additions. Add nutmeg, lemon rind and whiskey. Resift flour with salt into batter. Fold in thoroughly. Add fruit and fold in. Turn batter into a well-buttered 9-inch loaf pan. Bake in preheated 350° oven for about 2 to 2½ hours, or until tester comes out clean. Sprinkle with a little more whiskey while warm. Cool and store in an airtight container for 1 week before serving.

Makes 1 loaf cake

GOLDEN COCONUT FRUIT CAKE

[Southern United States]

1 cup (½ pound) unsalted butter
1¼ cups sugar
6 eggs
2 cups flour
¼ teaspoon powdered cloves
½ teaspoon each nutmeg and mace
2 teaspoons cinnamon
½ cup sherry
¼ cup rose water
½ pound each raisins, currants and coarsely chopped figs
½ pound citron, chopped
1 pound almonds, chopped
2½ cups grated unsweetened coconut (see note)

Cream butter and sugar together until light and fluffy. Add eggs, one at a time, beating well between additions. Reserve a little flour to dredge fruits. Sift remaining flour with spices. Gradually add combined sherry and rose water and flour alternately to the butter mixture, beating well between additions. Fold in floured fruits, almonds and coconut. Turn into two 8-inch loaf pans that are buttered and lined with buttered brown paper. Bake in preheated 275° oven for about 3½ hours, or until a tester comes out clean. Remove cakes, peel off paper, cool on a rack, wrap in foil or waxed paper and store in airtight containers.

Makes about 6 pounds of cake

Note: If you cannot get unsweetened coconut, use the sweetened type and only half the amount of sugar.

CHARLESTON CRYSTAL WHITE FRUIT CAKE

1½ pounds chopped citron
1½ pounds golden raisins
1½ pounds blanched almonds, ground
1 pound crystallized pineapple, diced
Meat of 1 fresh coconut, grated
4 cups flour
2 cups (1 pound) butter
2½ cups sugar
6 eggs
2 tablespoons nutmeg
1 cup sherry
2 tablespoons rose water
1 teaspoon almond extract
1½ tablespoons vanilla
2 recipes each Almond Paste Icing, page 206, and Royal Icing, page 207

Combine all fruits, almonds and coconut and sprinkle with a little flour, tossing mixture so all pieces are lightly coated. Cream butter with sugar until smooth. Add eggs, one at a time, beating well between additions. Sift remaining flour with spices and add, with sherry and flavorings, mixing well to blend. Fold in fruits and nuts. Turn the batter into two 9-inch loaf pans that have been buttered and lined with buttered brown paper. Bake at 250° for about 3 hours, or until a tester comes out clean. Peel off paper while warm, and cool completely. Spread with Almond Paste Icing, then cover with Royal Icing. This is best if it is not cut for at least one week.

Makes 2 loaf cakes

BLACK FRUIT CAKE

[*Southern United States, Italy and Canada*]

½ pound seedless black raisins
1 pound golden raisins
1 pound currants
½ cup dark rum, brandy, sherry or hard apple cider
½ pound each diced candied orange peel, lemon peel and citron
½ pound candied cherries, cut in half
½ pound candied pineapple, shredded
¼ pound blanched almonds, shredded
¼ pound walnuts, coarsely chopped
2 cups sifted flour
1 teaspoon baking soda
1 teaspoon cinnamon
1½ teaspoons allspice
½ teaspoon each nutmeg and mace
¼ teaspoon powdered cloves
1 cup (½ pound) unsalted butter
1 cup granulated sugar
1 cup firmly packed brown sugar
6 eggs
½ cup molasses
2 ounces (squares) semisweet chocolate, melted
1 cup strawberry or apricot preserves
Almond Paste Icing, page 206, and Royal Icing, page 207 (optional)

Soak raisins and currants in liquor overnight. Pour off and reserve liquor. Drain fruit on paper towel. Combine raisins with candied fruits and nuts and dredge lightly with ½ cup flour. Sift remaining flour with baking soda and spices. Cream butter with both sugars until light and fluffy. Add eggs one at a time, beating well between additions. Mix molasses, reserved liquor and melted chocolate and add to the batter alternately with the flour, beating well between additions. Fold in preserves and floured fruit.

Turn batter into three 9-inch loaf pans that are buttered and lined with buttered brown paper. Press batter down firmly with your hand. Bake in preheated 275° oven for about 4½ hours, or until a tester comes out clean. Cool in pan for 30 minutes, turn out onto rack, remove paper and cool completely. Store wrapped in rum- or brandy-soaked cloth and place in an airtight container. Serve plain or iced.

Makes about 6 pounds

JAMAICA BLACK FRUIT CAKE

The real secret of this cake lies in the soaking of the fruit in the rum—a process that should never take less than four weeks and is even better if it takes four months. In Jamaica, it is quite common for the mixture to be prepared in August. This recipe is adapted from a rare and wonderful old Jamaican book, *Cookie's Cookery Book.*

- **2 cups black raisins**
- **2 cups golden raisins**
- **3 cups currants**
- **1 cup diced citron**
- **1 cup dried figs, chopped**
- **¾ cup pitted chopped dates**
- **¾ cup cooked, pitted, drained and chopped prunes**
- **⅔ cup sliced brandied cherries**
- **¼ cup chopped candied orange peel**
- **½ cup chopped, toasted blanched almonds**
- **2 cups dark Jamaica rum**
- **¼ cup orange juice**
- **¼ cup brandy from cherries**
- **1 cup (½ pound) unsalted butter**
- **2 cups firmly packed dark brown sugar**
- **5 eggs**
- **2 cups flour**
- **2 teaspoons baking powder**
- **½ teaspoon each powdered cloves, cinnamon, nutmeg and allspice**
- **Pinch of salt**
- **Almond Paste Icing, page 206, and Royal Icing, page 207**

Combine all fruits and nuts. Cover with a mixture of rum, orange juice and cherry brandy, adding a little more of each if necessary to cover fruit completely. Cover loosely and set in a cool place to mellow as long as you like, but for no less than four weeks. Before baking, cream butter with sugar until light and fluffy. Add the eggs one at a time, beating well between additions. Sift flour twice with baking powder, spices and salt. Resift half of the flour into the butter mixture and blend in thoroughly. Add fruits with their soaking liquid and remaining flour and stir together very thoroughly.

Butter two 8-inch square cake pans or 9-inch loaf pans and line with buttered brown paper. Then turn batter into pans and bake in preheated 300° oven for 2 to 2½ hours, or until a tester comes out clean. Place a small pan half full of water on the bottom of oven for the first half of baking time to keep cake moist. Cool in pans for 1 hour, invert onto a rack and peel off paper. Moisten with a little more rum. Let dry and cool completely. Cover with Almond Paste Icing, then Royal Icing. Store in airtight container and allow to ripen 1 to 2 months.

Makes 2 cakes

Variation: Candied cherries and 1/4 cup kirsch or Cherry Heering can be substituted for brandied cherries.

MARTHA WASHINGTON'S GREAT CAKE

This rich fruit cake was traditionally served at Mount Vernon on Christmas, New Year's Day and Twelfth Night. The original recipe, now in the Mount Vernon archives, starts by calling for forty eggs, the whites to be beaten to froth with a bundle of twigs. This modern adaptation is reprinted from *The American Heritage Cookbook.*

1 pound golden raisins
1 box (11 ounces) currants
1 cup (8 ounces) candied orange peel
3/4 cup (6 ounces) candied lemon peel
1 cup (8 ounces) citron
1/3 cup (3 ounces) candied angelica
1/3 cup (3 ounces) candied red cherries
1/3 cup (3 ounces) candied green cherries
1/2 cup brandy
4 1/2 cups sifted all-purpose flour
1 teaspoon mace
1/2 teaspoon nutmeg
2 cups (1 pound) softened butter
2 cups sugar
10 eggs, separated
2 teaspoons fresh lemon juice
1/3 cup sherry

Pick over raisins and currants and soak them in water overnight. Chop orange and lemon peel quite fine; do the same with the citron, angelica and both kinds of cherries. Pour brandy over fruit, cover, and allow to stand overnight. The following day sift together flour, mace and nutmeg. Set aside. Work butter until creamy, then add 1 cup sugar, a little at a time, beating until smooth. Beat egg yolks until thick and light, then beat in remaining cup of sugar, a little at a time, and the lemon juice. Combine with butter-sugar mixture. Add flour and sherry alternately. Stir in all the fruit, and last of all, fold in stiffly beaten egg whites.

Pour the batter into a well-greased and floured 10-inch tube pan, a 10-inch Turk's-head mold, or 2 large loaf pans. Place pan of hot water in the bottom of a preheated 350° oven. Place cake pans in oven and bake for 20 minutes. Reduce heat to 325° and continue baking 1 hour and 40 minutes for large cake; 40 minutes for loaf cakes. Cakes are done when a toothpick, inserted at the center, comes out dry. Turn out on rack to cool, then wrap in cheesecloth soaked in sherry (or brandy) and store in an airtight crock or tin for a month or more. If during this mellowing period the cheesecloth dries out, soak it again with the same spirits and rewrap the cake.

Recipe makes about 11 pounds

ESTONIAN HONEY CAKE

[*Mee Kook*]

- 1 cup dark honey
- 1½ teaspoons cinnamon
- ½ teaspoon nutmeg
- ½ teaspoon powdered cardamom (optional)
- ½ cup (¼ pound) unsalted butter
- 1 cup sugar
- 6 egg yolks
- 2½ cups flour
- 2 teaspoons baking soda
- Pinch of salt
- Grated rind of 1 lemon
- ½ cup milk
- 6 egg whites stiffly beaten with 2 tablespoons sugar
- Fine dry bread crumbs
- 12 to 18 whole blanched almonds (optional)

Combine honey and spices and bring to a boil. Remove from heat and cool. Cream butter with sugar until very pale and fluffy. Add egg yolks and beat until smooth and well blended. Stir in cooled honey and spices. Sift flour with baking soda and salt. Add lemon rind. Resift flour into batter alternately with milk, beating well between each addition. Fold in stiffly beaten egg whites.

(continued)

This cake can be baked in a 9-inch fluted tube pan, a 9-inch loaf pan or a 10-inch round cake pan. Grease the pans with butter, sprinkle with bread crumbs and tap out excess. If you use a loaf pan or a cake pan, arrange almonds on top of the cake. Bake in preheated 375° oven for 40 minutes. Reduce heat to 325° and bake 20 minutes more, or until a tester comes out clean. Cool until cake shrinks from sides of pan. Turn out and cool on a rack. When completely cool, wrap well and let mellow for 2 days before cutting.

Makes 1 cake

OLD-FASHIONED DARK GINGERBREAD

[*Europe and United States*]

- **1⅓ cups flour**
- **1 teaspoon baking powder**
- **2 teaspoons ginger**
- **1 teaspoon cinnamon**
- **½ teaspoon powdered cloves**
- **½ teaspoon salt**
- **4 tablespoons unsalted butter, or 2 tablespoons butter and 2 tablespoons lard**
- **¼ cup light brown sugar, firmly packed**
- **1 egg**
- **½ cup boiling water**
- **½ cup dark molasses**
- **½ teaspoon baking soda**
- **½ cup chopped black walnuts (optional)**
- **Confectioners' sugar or whipped cream**

Sift flour with baking powder, spices and salt and set aside. Cream shortening with sugar until light and fluffy; add egg and beat thoroughly; combine boiling water and molasses, stir in soda until dissolved and add to batter. Resift flour mixture and add gradually, stirring well between additions. Add nuts. Pour into a well-buttered 8-inch square pan, or an 8-inch loaf pan. Bake in preheated 350° oven for 20 to 30 minutes, or until a tester comes out clean. Cool until cake shrinks from sides of pan. Invert onto a rack, cool completely and sprinkle with confectioners' sugar or top with whipped cream before serving.

Makes 1 cake

IRISH FRUITED GINGERBREAD

Follow basic recipe, page 64. Substitute mace and allspice for cloves and ginger. After adding flour, stir in a scant ¼ cup washed and dried raisins, 2 tablespoons chopped mixed candied fruit peel and 2 tablespoons chopped blanched almonds.

PAIN D'ÉPICE

[*France*]

Dijon is one of France's greatest gastronomic meccas, and the local spice bread is one of the reasons. Similar breads are also made in Belgium and Holland.

1 cup dark honey
1 cup sugar
1 tablespoon baking soda
1 cup hot water (boiled, not from the tap)
1 tablespoon crushed anise seeds
Grated rind of 1 orange or 1½ lemons
Pinch of salt
1 cup rye flour
3 cups unbleached flour
½ cup hot milk

Combine honey, sugar and baking soda in water that is hot but not boiling. Blend well. Stir in anise seeds, rind and salt, sift in flour gradually, beating well between additions. To be at its best, batter should age from 3 to 8 days in a cool place. (You may eliminate this step if you lack patience or time, but it does greatly improve the flavor.) Turn batter into 2 well buttered 7-inch loaf pans. Bake in preheated 350° oven for 1 hour. Brush with hot milk as soon as it comes from the oven.

Makes 2 loaf cakes

Variations: A quarter of a cup of finely chopped candied orange rind is sometimes added instead of the fresh rind.

A little dry mustard—about ½ teaspoon—is often added with the anise.

Thin slices may be sandwiched together with orange marmalade; or serve sliced and buttered.

PRINTEN

The city called Aix-la-Chapelle in French and Aachen in German is known for a type of Pain d'Épice called Printen. It is made in either of two ways (both based on the above recipe). The first, molded Printen, uses extra flour to make a dough smooth enough to roll. It is then stamped with Springerle or Printen molds (which range from a few inches up to 3 feet long), and baked on a cookie sheet. The second and simpler version is Printen slices, for which the batter is spread on a cookie sheet about 1½ inches thick. After it is baked it is cut into finger strips and left plain or iced with chocolate. Cloves, ginger, allspice, crushed rock candy, cinnamon and pepper may be added, to taste.

SCANDINAVIAN GINGERBREAD

[*Pepparkakor*]

This dark and moist gingerbread is a personal favorite.

1⅔ cups flour
1 teaspoon baking soda
Pinch of salt
1 scant teaspoon crushed cardamom (optional)
2 teaspoons cinnamon
½ teaspoon cloves
1 teaspoon ginger
1 cup sugar (white or firmly packed brown)
½ cup (¼ pound) unsalted butter
2 eggs
¾ cup sour cream
⅓ cup raisins or currants (optional)
Fine, dry bread crumbs

Sift flour with baking soda, salt and spices and set aside. Cream sugar and butter until light and fluffy. Add eggs, one at a time, beating well between additions. Resift flour in gradually, alternating with sour cream and beating well between additions. Fold in raisins or currants. Butter a 9-inch loaf pan, a 9-inch square pan or a 9-inch fluted tube pan and sprinkle inside with fine bread crumbs, tapping excess out. Turn batter into pan and bake in preheated

325° oven for 45 minutes to 1 hour, or until a tester comes out clean. Cool until cake shrinks from sides of pan, then invert onto a rack and cool completely.

Makes 1 cake

OATMEAL GINGERBREAD

[*Scotland*]

2 cups flour
1 tablespoon powdered ginger
1 teaspoon baking soda
Pinch of salt
2 cups instant oatmeal
¼ cup finely chopped candied lemon peel (optional)
⅔ cup golden molasses
½ cup (¼ pound) unsalted butter
1 cup firmly packed brown sugar
2 eggs, well beaten
⅓ to ½ cup buttermilk, as needed

Sift together flour, ginger, soda and salt; mix with oatmeal and lemon peel. Bring molasses to a boil and add butter and sugar. Remove from heat and stir until butter melts and sugar dissolves. Cool and mix with beaten eggs. Pour into the flour mixture, beating vigorously until well blended. Add just enough buttermilk to make a batter that can be dropped from a spoon. Turn into a well-buttered 10″ × 12″ × 3″ baking pan and bake in preheated 325° oven for about 2 hours, or until a tester comes out clean. If cake browns too quickly, cover with buttered brown paper or double thickness of aluminum foil, and continue baking.

Makes 1 cake

UKRAINIAN HONEY CAKE

[*Medivnyk*]

- **1 cup dark honey**
- **1 teaspoon powdered cinnamon**
- **½ teaspoon nutmeg or mace**
- **½ teaspoon powdered cloves**
- **½ cup (¼ pound) softened unsalted butter**
- **2 teaspoons baking soda**
- **1 cup dark brown sugar, firmly packed**
- **5 egg yolks**
- **4 cups sifted flour**
- **½ teaspoon salt**
- **1½ teaspoons baking powder**
- **¾ cup golden raisins**
- **½ cup currants**
- **⅓ cup chopped pitted dates**
- **3 tablespoons chopped candied orange peel**
- **1 cup chopped walnuts or blanched almonds**
- **5 egg whites stiffly beaten with 1 tablespoon sugar**

Combine honey and spices, bring to a boil, remove from heat and cool. Cream butter with baking soda and sugar until light and fluffy. Add egg yolks, one at a time, beating well between additions. Resift flour with salt and baking powder. Add flour and honey to butter mixture and stir in thoroughly. Mix in fruits and nuts. Fold in stiffly beaten egg whites. Pour into two 7- or 8-inch loaf pans that have been buttered and lined with buttered brown paper. Bake in preheated 325° oven for 2 to 2½ hours, or until a tester comes out clean. Turn out of pans, remove paper, cool and let mellow for 2 days before cutting.

Makes 2 loaf cakes

GINGERBREAD LAYER CAKE

[*United States and Europe*]

Filled with clouds of whipped cream, this cake was Abraham Lincoln's favorite Christmas dessert.

1 cup dark honey
1 teaspoon ginger
1 teaspoon cinnamon
½ teaspoon powdered cloves
2½ cups sifted flour
1 teaspoon baking powder
½ teaspoon salt
½ cup (¼ pound) unsalted butter
1 teaspoon baking soda
½ cup light brown sugar, firmly packed
Grated rind of 1 lemon
1 egg
1 cup buttermilk
2 cups lightly sweetened whipped cream, grated rind of 1 orange, ½ cup grated semi-sweet chocolate

Combine honey and spices, bring to a boil, remove from heat and cool. Sift flour with baking powder and salt. Cream butter with baking soda and sugar until light and fluffy. Add lemon rind and egg and mix thoroughly. Add flour and buttermilk alternately to butter mixture, stirring well between additions. Pour into 2 well-buttered and floured 8-inch square pans. Bake in preheated 350° oven for about 35 minutes, or until a tester comes out clean. Cool in pans until cakes shrink from sides. Turn out onto rack and cool completely. Spread one layer with half of the whipped cream. Top with second layer. Spread with remaining cream and sprinkle with orange rind and chocolate. Chill 2 or 3 hours before serving.

Makes 1 two-layer cake

HONEY-NUT FORTUNE CAKE

[*Yugoslavia—Cesnica; Greece, Armenia, The Levant—Baklava*]

The person who finds the coin in his portion is supposed to enjoy good fortune in the year ahead.

1 1-pound package strudel or Greek phyllo leaves
¾ to 1 cup melted unsalted butter, as needed
1 cup coarsely ground walnuts
½ to 1 cup golden raisins
1 silver coin
1 cup honey
½ cup water
1 tablespoon lemon juice
1-inch stick cinnamon

Butter a 12-inch round baking dish that is 2 to 3 inches deep. Place in it three layers of strudel or phyllo leaves, brushing each with a little melted butter before adding the next. Sprinkle with nuts and a few raisins. Top with a single sheet of pastry, brush with butter and add more nuts and raisins. Continue alternating single sheets of buttered pastry with the filling until the pan is almost full. Top with a triple layer of buttered pastry leaves, without filling. The stack should be about 2 inches thick.

Trim edges of dough to fit circular pan. Pack pastry down lightly by pressing it with your hands. Place a small juice glass or cookie cutter upside down in the center of the cake. Using a sharp pointed knife, cut around the glass and through all of the layers of pastry and filling. Remove glass or cookie cutter. Slip a foil-wrapped silver coin between any two layers of pastry. Score a diamond pattern out from the circle, all over the top of the cake. Pour ½ cup melted butter over the top. Bake in preheated 350° oven for 20 to 30 minutes, or until golden brown.

Meanwhile, cook honey and water with lemon juice and cinnamon until the mixture forms a syrup. Remove cinnamon and pour hot syrup over the cake as soon as it is removed from the oven. Cool to room temperature and serve.

Lay pretty long in bed, and then rose, leaving my wife desirous to sleep, having sat up till four this morning seeing her maid make mince pies . . .

Samuel Pepys, December 25th, 1666

MINCE PIE

Chopped beef and suet, cooked and preserved with dried fruits, nuts, spices and spiked with brandy or wine, has been the filling for English Christmas pies since medieval days. Mincemeat can be preserved indefinitely, and if you make a large batch of it, it is best to put it up in pie-size quantities so you can open only as much as you need. Two to three cups of filling is enough for an 8-inch pie; plan on three to four cups for a 9-inch pie.

1 recipe Epiphany Jam Tart pastry, page 80 or
1 recipe Scots Black Bun pastry, page 74
3 to 4 cups mincemeat filling of your choice

If you want to make a two-crust pie, which is traditional for this recipe, use the full amount of pastry. If you prefer a lattice crust, make a little more than half the amount called for. Roll pie crust out to fit a 9-inch round pie plate. Place in unbuttered pan if you use the first pastry, or in a buttered pan if you use the second. Fill with mincemeat. Cover with top crust or lattice strips and bake in a preheated 400° oven for about 45 minutes, or until crust is golden brown. Crust may be sprinkled with sugar halfway through baking, or it can be glazed with a mixture of 1 egg yolk beaten with 2 tablespoons milk before being baked.

Makes 1 pie

OLD ENGLISH MINCEMEAT

- 1½ pounds lean beef, cut in 1-inch cubes
- ¾ pound beef suet, ground
- 6 medium-size tart apples, peeled and chopped
- 3 cups brown sugar, firmly packed
- ½ cup molasses
- 2 cups apple cider
- 1½ pounds currants
- ¾ pound golden raisins
- ¾ pound black raisins
- ½ cup diced citron
- ½ cup diced candied orange peel
- Juice and ground or chopped rind of 1½ lemons
- 1 teaspoon each powdered coriander, allspice, nutmeg, mace, cloves and cinnamon
- ¾ pound shelled walnuts, or blanched almonds, coarsely chopped
- ¾ cup sherry or rum
- ¾ cup brandy or whiskey

Boil cubed beef in a little beef stock or water for about 30 minutes, or until it is soft enough to pull apart into shreds. Combine shredded beef, ground suet, apples, sugar, molasses and cider and bring to a boil. Add currants, raisins, candied fruits and lemon and cook for 30 minutes, stirring frequently until mixture is thick. Stir in spices and simmer until liquid is reduced and mixture is very thick. Fold in nuts, sherry or rum and brandy or whiskey.

Mixture is now ready to use for pies. Or if you want to preserve it, pack into sterilized jars, adjust lids and process in hot-water bath for 1½ hours. Seal and use as needed.

Makes about 4 quarts, or enough for four to five 8- to 9-inch pies

Variations: Cooked and shredded fresh beef tongue is often substituted for the beef or used in combination with it.

Use a half-and-half combination of quince and apples.

Cook and shred the beef and mix with the other ingredients, eliminating the cider, and without cooking any further, age the mixture for 3 weeks in a crock set in a cool place. Taste and add spices, salt or sugar as needed, and age a week more before using.

Substitute dried or candied fruits, such as apricots, cherries or pineapple, to taste, for some of the dried and candied fruits called for.

MEATLESS MINCEMEAT

- 1 seeded orange
- 1 seeded lemon
- 1½ cups golden raisins
- 1½ cups currants
- 8 tart apples
- ¾ cup mixed candied diced fruit peel
- 1¾ cups apple cider
- 3½ cups firmly packed dark brown sugar
- 1 teaspoon salt
- 1½ teaspoons each powdered coriander, cinnamon, allspice, mace, nutmeg and cloves
- Brandy or whiskey, optional and to taste
- Rum or sherry, optional and to taste

Using the coarse blade of a food chopper, grind cut-up seeded orange and lemon (with rinds) and raisins, currants, cored but unpeeled apples and candied fruit. Add cider, bring to a boil and simmer, uncovered, for 15 minutes or until fairly dry. Add sugar, salt and spices and simmer 10 to 15 minutes longer, or until thick. Stir in brandy or whiskey and rum or sherry to taste. Use at once, or process as in preceding recipe.

Makes enough for three to four 9-inch pies

GREEN TOMATO MINCEMEAT

[*Pennsylvania Dutch*]

- 12 green tomatoes
- 12 tart apples
- 1½ cups currants
- 1½ cups golden raisins
- 4 cups brown sugar, firmly packed
- ½ cup cider vinegar
- 1 tablespoon cinnamon
- 1 teaspoon each powdered cloves, allspice and nutmeg
- ½ teaspoon black pepper
- 2 teaspoons salt
- ½ cup ground suet

Chop tomatoes. Peel, core and chop apples. Cover tomatoes with water, bring to a boil, drain and repeat twice more, using fresh water for each boiling. Drain well after the third boiling and combine with all ingredients. Bring to a boil and simmer gently until mixture is thick and liquid has evaporated. Use at once, or process as in Old English Mincemeat (page 70).

Makes about 2 to 3 quarts, enough for three or four 8- to 9-inch pies

SCOTS BLACK BUN

A sort of plum pudding pie, this is served in Scotland on Hogmanay —New Year's Eve.

PASTRY:

3 cups flour
Pinch of salt
¾ cup unsalted butter
2 to 3 tablespoons ice water, as needed

FILLING:

3 cups currants
3 cups golden raisins, chopped
1¼ cups mixed diced candied fruit peel
1¼ cups chopped blanched almonds
3 cups flour
2 teaspoons powdered ginger
½ teaspoon powdered cloves
1 teaspoon cinnamon
¼ teaspoon black pepper
¾ teaspoon baking soda
¾ cup light brown sugar, firmly packed
2 eggs, beaten
1 tablespoon brandy
¾ cup buttermilk, as needed

1 egg yolk beaten with 1 tablespoon cold water

Sift flour and salt together. Cut in butter with two knives or a pastry blender until mixture resembles fine meal. Add just enough water to make dough stick together. Knead for a minute or two until smooth. Roll two thirds of the dough into a thin circle that will fit a 9- or 10-inch pie plate. Roll out remaining dough to form a cover. Line a buttered pan with the bottom piece of dough. (A less authentic but very good alternate dough for this is the one used in the following recipe.)

Combine all fruits and nuts. Sift flour with spices and baking soda. Add sugar to fruit mixture. Sift in flour. Toss until all ingredients are thoroughly mixed. Add eggs, brandy and just enough buttermilk to form a very thick paste. Turn into pie plate, moisten edges of crust and cover with top pie crust, crimping the edges closed. Using a long skewer, make four holes down through the filling and bottom crust; then prick additional holes in the top crust with the tines of a fork. Bake in preheated 350° oven for 3 hours. Brush with egg yolk glaze for last hour of baking. If you can bear to wait, this black bun will taste much better if you let it mellow 3 or 4 days before serving.

SICILIAN MARSALA FIG CAKE

[*Cucidata*]

PASTRY:

- 6 cups flour
- 1 teaspoon baking powder
- 1 teaspoon salt
- 1 cup sugar
- Grated rind of ½ lemon
- ¾ cup lard or vegetable shortening
- 1 cup unsalted butter
- 4 tablespoons brandy
- ½ cup ice water, as needed

FILLING:

- 2 cups seedless dark raisins
- 1½ pounds dried figs
- Rind of 1 orange and of 1 lemon
- ½ pound blanched, toasted almonds
- ½ pound shelled walnuts
- ⅔ cup Marsala wine
- 2 teaspoons cinnamon
- 1 tablespoon lightly crushed fennel seeds

Sift dry pastry ingredients into bowl. Add lemon rind and cut in lard and butter, using two knives or a pastry blender, until mixture resembles fine meal. Add brandy and gradually add water, meanwhile tossing mixture with a fork. Add only enough water to make a pastry that holds together. Knead 2 or 3 minutes and chill for 45 minutes.

Using the coarse blade of your food chopper, grind together raisins, figs, fruit rind and nuts. Add wine gradually to help mixture go through the grinder. Mix in cinnamon and fennel.

Divide dough into 4 parts. Roll each part out to a long narrow rectangle about ⅛ inch thick. Trim rectangle into 4½-inch-wide strips. The finished rings can range from 4 to 14 inches in diameter, so cut strips to the length required for the size you want. Spoon a 1-inch-wide, ½-inch-thick strip of fruit filling down the center of each piece of dough. Fold dough over filling to close roll, pinching edges closed. Flip over so seam is on bottom. Press sides of roll to make it high and thin. Trim ends and draw together to form a circle. Using the tines of a fork, prick rows of holes around the sides and over the top of the rim at ¾-inch intervals. Or slash diagonally with a knife at intervals all around the ring. Place on buttered baking sheet and bake in preheated 375° oven for 20 minutes, or until pale golden brown. Cool before serving.

Makes 3 or 4 medium-sized rings

PANFORTE DI SIENA

[*Italy*]

The "strong bread" is practically a confection, similar to Torrone or nougat candy. It has been a Christmas specialty of Siena since the Renaissance and is exported to all parts of the world each year.

½ cup each minced candied orange rind, lemon rind and citron
¼ cup brandy
1 tablespoon flour
¾ cup blanched toasted almonds
¾ cup toasted hazelnuts, with skins rubbed off
2 tablespoons unsweetened cocoa
2 teaspoons cinnamon
¼ teaspoon allspice
1 cup dark honey
2 cups sugar
⅓ cup sifted flour
Bakers' rice wafers, page 242 (optional)
Cinnamon
Confectioners' sugar

Soak candied fruits in brandy for 1 hour. Drain and reserve both fruits and brandy. Dredge fruit lightly with flour. Split almonds and hazelnuts into halves. Mix with fruit, cocoa and spices. Combine honey with sugar and reserved brandy in a small heavy-bottomed saucepan. Boil until mixture forms a hard ball when dropped into cold water, or until it reaches 243° on a candy thermometer. Combine hot syrup with nuts and cocoa mixture, stirring vigorously until nuts and fruits are well distributed.

If you are using wafers, butter a 9-inch round layer-cake pan and line with a wafer. If not, butter a pan and line it with buttered waxed paper. Pour mixture into pan, leveling it with the back of a spoon. Top with a wafer if you are using them. Otherwise, do not cover with anything. Bake in preheated 275° oven for 20 to 30 minutes, or until mixture is firm. Cool in pan and sprinkle with cinnamon and sugar before serving. This will keep for a long time if it is well wrapped and stored in an airtight container. If it is left open it will become hard as a rock in a day.

Makes 1 nine-inch cake

PEPPERED BREAD

[*Panpepato*]

Neither bread nor peppered, this a derivation of Panforte di Siena (above) made in the Emilia section of Italy. It is prepared in much the same manner as in the preceding recipe, but is spread with a chocolate icing (see pages 203–205) after it has been cooled and turned out of the pan.

CERTOSINO

This version of Panforte takes its name from a wine of the area with which it is made. It is a New Year's Day specialty of Bologna.

Follow recipe for Panforte di Siena, page 78, substituting a dry robust red wine (preferably Certosino) for the brandy. Use 1½ cups almonds and eliminate hazelnuts. Substitute powdered cloves for allspice and add ½ teaspoon nutmeg. When batter is in pan, on wafer or not, decorate the top with strips of candied fruit peel, candied cherry halves and whole blanched untoasted almonds. Bake as described.

EPIPHANY JAM TART

[*England*]

Jams of all colors create the effect of stained glass in this Victorian specialty.

4 to 4½ cups flour
½ teaspoon salt
⅔ cup sugar
½ teaspoon cinnamon
1½ cups (¾ pound) unsalted butter, slightly softened
2 eggs
4 hard-boiled egg yolks, sieved
2 to 4 tablespoons milk, white wine or vinegar
Grated rind of 1 lemon

Different-colored thick jams (see below)
1 egg yolk beaten with 1 tablespoon milk

Sift 4 cups flour with salt, sugar and cinnamon into a wide bowl. Cut slightly softened butter into flour with two knives or a pastry blender until mixture is the texture of fine meal. Combine eggs, yolks, liquid, and lemon rind. Form a well in center of flour, add mixed ingredients, and using your fingertips, or a fork, work ingredients together until dough sticks together in a ball. Add a little more flour or liquid if needed. Knead dough for a minute or two until smooth. Wrap in waxed paper and chill for 30 minutes.

Roll out half the dough between sheets of waxed paper to fit a 9-inch pie plate; dough to be about ¼ inch thick. Fit into ungreased pie plate. Roll out remaining dough in a circle of the same size. From this, cut a 1-inch ring that will fit around the edge of the

pie plate. Cut remaining dough into strips to form the pattern. This may be done in long strips or by piecing together shorter strips. Reknead and reroll scraps if necessary. Arrange strips of dough across top of pie plate, as shown, and cover with ring of pastry.

Carefully spoon as many different-colored jams as possible into the spaces between the lattice strips, using prune (lekvar), strawberry, raspberry, gooseberry, orange marmalade, quince and pineapple preserves, damson or greengage plum, etc. Brush dough strips with egg yolk glaze and bake in preheated 350° oven for 30 to 45 minutes.

Makes 1 nine-inch tart.

FINNISH SOUR CREAM CAKE

[*Kermakakku*]

A wonderfully dry bland cake, not too rich, that is a must on every Finnish holiday sweet table.

¾ cup flour
¾ cup potato flour or starch
1 teaspoon baking powder
½ teaspoon baking soda
Pinch of salt
1 cup sour cream
1 cup sugar
1 egg, beaten
Grated rind of 1 lemon, or 1 teaspoon vanilla, or 2 teaspoons brandy
Fine dry bread crumbs
Vanilla Sugar (confectioners'), page 211

Sift flours with baking powder, soda and salt. Beat sour cream until smooth and then mix with sugar, egg and flavoring. Resift dry ingredients into sour cream batter and mix until thoroughly blended. Turn into an 8-inch fluted tube pan that has been well buttered and lightly sprinkled with bread crumbs. Bake in preheated 350° oven for 45 minutes to 1 hour, or until golden brown and a tester comes out clean. Cool until cake shrinks from sides of pan. Invert onto a rack to continue cooling. Sprinkle with sugar before serving.

Makes 1 eight-inch cake

BÛCHE DE NOËL

This creamy mocha Christmas Log is France's best-known and most festive holiday specialty and is always on the table for the Réveillon supper, held just after midnight Mass on Christmas Eve. It is also served on New Year's Eve, and the number of the new year is written on the log with decorative icing. This same cake is popular in northern Italy, where it is called Ceppo di Natale.

SPONGE SHEET:

- 1 cup cake flour, sifted
- Pinch of baking powder
- Pinch of salt
- 4 egg yolks
- 1 cup sugar
- ½ teaspoon vanilla extract
- 4 egg whites
- 1 tablespoon sugar

- Rum
- Confectioners' sugar

MOCHA BUTTER CREAM:

- ½ cup water
- 1¼ cups sugar
- 5 egg yolks
- 1½ cups (¾ pound) unsalted butter
- 2 ounces unsweetened chocolate, melted and cooled
- 2 teaspoons instant coffee powder

- Decorative Sugar Icing, page 207, marzipan tinted with green coloring, almonds, sprigs of holly, green sugar, chopped pistachio nuts, candied cherries, etc.

Sift flour twice with baking powder and salt. Beat yolks with 1 cup of sugar and vanilla until very thick and pale yellow. Beat egg whites, and as they begin to stiffen, add 1 tablespoon sugar. Beat until whites hold stiff peaks. Sift flour onto yolk mixture a little at a time and fold in between additions. Add whites and fold in gently but thoroughly, using a rubber spatula.

Pour into a 10″ × 15″ jelly-roll pan that is buttered and lined with buttered waxed paper. Spread evenly over pan and bake in preheated 400° oven for 12 to 15 minutes, or until cake is light golden brown. Sprinkle with rum. Spread a sheet of waxed paper on the counter top and sprinkle with confectioners' sugar. Invert cake onto sugar and gently draw off paper. Trim off crusty edges. Gently roll cake with the paper, jelly-roll fashion, starting with a long edge. Cool for 20 minutes.

Meanwhile, prepare butter cream. Combine water and sugar and boil until mixture forms a soft ball when a little is dropped into ice water, or until it reaches 238° on a candy thermometer. Beat egg yolks until pale yellow and thick and slowly pour in hot syrup, beating constantly. Continue beating until mixture is cool. Beat in butter, a little at a time, then add remaining ingredients. If cream has softened too much, place in refrigerator until firm.

Unroll cake and spread with half the cream. Reroll filled cake (without paper) as firmly as possible without breaking it and chill several hours, keeping remaining butter cream cool. Trim off ends of cake on a slant and save small pieces for decorative touches. Spread roll with remaining cream, then with a spatula or fork, score a rough barklike surface onto frosting or force through a pastry tube. Cut reserved scraps of cake into knots and branches. Frost with butter cream and place on and alongside cake. Decorate with marzipan leaves, almonds, cherries or swirls of colored icing, in any combination you like. Ends of cake may be covered with finely chopped pistachio nuts, green marzipan or colored sugar.

Makes 8 to 10 servings

LITHUANIAN BIRCH LOG

[*Berzo Saka*]

Follow preceding recipe. When cake is unrolled, spread with a thick paste of 2 cups warm prune jam (lekvar) mixed with 1 cup of butter that has been creamed with ½ cup sugar. Stir in 1 square of melted semisweet chocolate, ½ cup chopped walnuts, grated rind of ½ orange, 2 egg yolks and 1 teaspoon vanilla or 1 tablespoon rum. Reroll, and when firm, spread with Fondant Icing, page 203. Use a chocolate icing, pages 203–205, to make lines imitating birch bark.

ENGLISH YULE LOG

Follow basic recipe, page 82. When cake is unrolled, spread with warm melted apricot jam and chopped blanched almonds. Roll and spread with red currant jelly, then Almond Paste Icing, page 206, and a chocolate icing, pages 203–205. Cover ends with chocolate. Use Decorative Sugar Icing, page 207, for markings.

NORWEGIAN YULE LOG

[*Julestamme*]

Follow basic recipe, page 82. Sprinkle warm cake with a little orange juice and roll. Unroll and spread with melted warm strawberry or raspberry jam. Roll and chill. Cover with whipped cream piped from a pastry tube, or spread with Almond Paste Icing, page 206. Cover ends and top with a chocolate icing, pages 203–205.

COOKIES & SMALL CAKES

Chapter Three

Drop and Bar Cookies

BRANDY SNAPS

[*England*]

Originally made as a *gaufrette* (small wafer) on a hot griddle, this recipe evolved to the baked cookies below. They are similar to the German Hippen, which are rolled and filled with butter cream.

1½ cups flour, sifted
Pinch of salt
2 teaspoons powdered ginger
1 teaspoon nutmeg
¾ cup unsalted butter, melted
1 cup brown sugar, firmly packed
½ cup dark molasses
2 tablespoons brandy

Resift flour with salt, ginger and nutmeg. Combine melted butter, sugar, molasses and brandy. Stir into dry ingredients. Drop by teaspoonfuls onto lightly buttered cookie sheet, leaving 2½ inches between cookies. Bake in preheated 300° oven for 10 to 15 minutes. Let cool only until cookies can be handled. While warm, roll each around the handle of a wooden mixing spoon to form "cigarettes." Reheat cookies in slow oven if they harden before they are rolled. Cool completely and store in airtight container. Cookies can also be shaped into cones, which may be filled with a mixture of whipped cream and chopped candied ginger just before serving.

Makes about 4 dozen cookies

ANISE DROPS

[*Germany—Anislaibchen*]

4 eggs
1¼ cups sugar
3 cups sifted flour
1¼ tablespoons lightly crushed anise seeds

Beat eggs with sugar until mixture is very thick and almost white. Resift flour and add gradually, blending well between additions. Stir in anise seeds. Heat a cookie sheet lightly and butter it, then chill it until completely cold. Drop dough from a teaspoon onto the cookie sheet, leaving 1 inch between cookies. Let dry uncovered, at room temperature, overnight. Bake in preheated 300° oven for about 20 minutes, or until pale golden.

Makes about 7 dozen cookies

APIES

[*Pennsylvania Dutch*]

These cookies were first made by Ann Page, a well-known local cook who used to stamp her initials A.P. on the cookies, thus giving them their name.

¾ cup unsalted butter
1½ cups sugar
2 eggs, well beaten
2½ cups flour
½ teaspoon baking soda
Pinch of salt
⅓ cup sour cream

Cream butter and sugar until light and fluffy. Beat in eggs thoroughly. Sift flour with baking soda and salt. Stir into batter gradually, alternating with sour cream and stirring well after each addition. Drop from a teaspoon onto a buttered cookie sheet. Bake in preheated 350° oven for about 10 minutes, or until cookies are crisp and sand-colored.

Makes about 5½ dozen cookies.

CANADIAN FRUIT SQUARES

- ½ cup walnuts, chopped
- ½ cup blanched almonds, chopped
- ¾ cup shredded coconut
- ¼ cup diced angelica
- ¼ cup diced candied orange peel
- ½ cup chopped red candied cherries
- 1 15-ounce can sweetened condensed milk
- 2 tablespoons flour
- 1 tablespoon unsweetened cocoa (optional)
- 1 to 2 tablespoons rye whiskey

Combine all ingredients and mix thoroughly. Pour into a well-buttered 9″ × 12″ pan. Bake in preheated 350° oven for 45 minutes, or until firm. Cut into 1½-inch squares.

Makes about 5 dozen cookies

VICTORIAN COCONUT GINGERSNAPS

[*England*]

- 1½ cups dark corn syrup
- ½ cup (¼ pound) unsalted butter
- ⅔ cup sugar
- 1½ cups rice flour or cornstarch, sifted
- 2½ cups flour, sifted
- 1 tablespoon powdered ginger
- ½ teaspoon salt
- 1½ teaspoons baking powder
- Grated rind of 1 lemon
- 2 tablespoons minced candied lemon peel
- 2 tablespoons minced candied orange peel
- 2 cups flaked coconut, preferably fresh and unsweetened

Heat corn syrup to boiling point, stir in butter and sugar. When butter melts, remove from heat. Resift rice flour or cornstarch with flour, ginger, salt and baking powder. Stir gradually into hot syrup. Add lemon rind and fruit peel. Cool mixture to lukewarm and stir in coconut. Let mixture stand until completely cold. Drop from two teaspoons onto a buttered baking sheet, leaving 2 inches between cookies. Bake in preheated 350° oven for about 25 minutes, or until cookies are golden brown around the edge and paler gold in the center.

Makes about 4 dozen cookies

The ancient Bavarian city, Nuremberg, famous for Albrecht Dürer and Hans Sachs, is even better known for these spicy cakes called Lebkuchen. They may be cut into any size or shape—rectangles, fingers and rounds being the usual forms. "Leb" is derived from the Latin libum, *a consecrated cake used in Roman religious ceremonies, hence they are, in German, sacred cakes.*

ELISE LEBKUCHEN

5 eggs
1 pound dark brown sugar
1 pound grated unblanched almonds
½ cup chopped citron
½ cup chopped candied orange peel
¼ teaspoon each powdered cloves, cardamom and nutmeg
1 tablespoon cinnamon
Grated rind of 1 lemon
40 small round bakers' rice wafers, page 242, White Sugar Glaze, page 206, or a chocolate icing, pages 203–205

Beat eggs and sugar until thick and pale yellow. Fold in almonds, fruit, peel, spices and lemon rind. Stir well. Spread in mounds onto wafers and arrange on a lightly buttered baking sheet. Let dry uncovered, at room temperature, overnight. Bake in preheated 300° oven for about 30 minutes, or until deep golden brown.

If you are using the glaze, brush on at once; but cool cookies completely before applying icing. Cut into rectangles when cool.

Makes about 3 dozen cookies

HONEY LEBKUCHEN

- 1 pound honey
- ¾ cup sugar
- 3 eggs
- ½ cup grated unblanched almonds or hazelnuts
- ¼ cup chopped citron
- ¼ cup chopped candied orange peel
- 1 teaspoon cinnamon
- ½ teaspoon powdered cloves
- 1 teaspoon lightly crushed anise seeds
- 1 cup strong black coffee or 1 cup milk
- 4½ cups flour
- 1½ teaspoons baking powder
- White Sugar Glaze, page 206; or a chocolate icing, pages 203–205; or paper cookie stickers, page 243

Heat honey until thin and slightly darkened in color. Stir in sugar until dissolved. Cool and beat in eggs, nuts, fruit and spices. Stir in coffee for cookies with a dark, richer flavor or milk if you prefer milder golden-colored cookies. Sift flour with baking powder and stir gradually into mixture. Blend thoroughly. (Dough can be baked now or you can allow it to age by placing it in a bowl, covering it and storing it in a cool place for 1 day to 1 week.) Spread dough about ½ inch thick on a lightly buttered and floured baking sheet. Bake in preheated 400° oven for 12 to 15 minutes, or until a deep golden brown. If you are using the glaze or stickers, add immediately, but cool cookies before covering with icing. Cut into rectangles when cool.

Makes about 3 dozen cookies

WHITE LEBKUCHEN

- 5 eggs
- 2½ cups sugar
- ½ cup grated blanched almonds
- ¼ cup chopped citron
- ¼ cup chopped candied orange peel
- Grated rind of 1 lemon
- 3 to 5 cups flour, as needed
- ¼ teaspoon each powdered cardamom and nutmeg
- ¼ teaspoon each powdered cinnamon and cloves (optional)
- 1 teaspoon baking powder

Beat eggs with sugar until thick and pale yellow. Add almonds, fruit, peel and lemon rind. Sift flour with spices and baking powder and add gradually to egg mixture, stirring well between additions. Add enough flour to make a fairly stiff dough that is not sticky. Knead on a floured board until smooth. Shape into finger-thick rolls; then cut in 1-inch slices. Arrange on a buttered cookie sheet and let dry uncovered, at room temperature, overnight. Bake in preheated 300° oven for about 20 minutes, or until pale golden brown.

Makes about 3 dozen cookies

Variation: If you would like to prepare these cookies with bakers' rice wafers, page 242, use 8 eggs to make a soft spreadable dough. Do not knead, but spread onto wafers, let dry overnight and then bake. This softer mixture can also be spread into a buttered 11″ × 16″ jelly-roll pan, then dried and baked. When still warm, cut into rectangles and cool thoroughly in pan before serving.

Although they are favorites throughout the year, macaroons are especially popular during the Christmas season throughout most of Europe.

HAZELNUT MACAROONS

2 egg whites from extra-large eggs
1 cup sifted confectioners' sugar
2 cups (¾ pound) ground unblanched hazelnuts
1 teaspoon cinnamon
18 whole unblanched hazelnuts

Beat egg whites to stiff glossy peaks. Combine sugar, ground nuts and cinnamon. Fold into whites. Butter and flour a baking sheet. Drop mixture onto pan, using two teaspoons; leave about 1 inch between cookies. Set a whole hazelnut in the center of each and let stand uncovered for 5 to 7 hours in a warm room. Bake in preheated 350° oven for 15 to 20 minutes, or until golden brown.

Makes about 1½ dozen cookies

ALMOND MACAROONS

Follow above recipe, using 2 egg whites, ¾ cup granulated sugar, ¾ cup grated unblanched almonds, ½ teaspoon almond extract and the grated rind of ½ lemon. Omit cinnamon. Dry and bake as directed.

PINE NUT MACAROONS

[*Italy—Pinoccate*]

Follow preceding recipe, or work enough confectioners' sugar into almond paste, purchased or made (page 165), to give a smooth dough that can be rolled in your hands. When macaroons are shaped and on baking sheet, stud generously with pine nuts. Let dry overnight, then bake. In Italy one often sees these macaroons sandwiched in pairs with apricot jam. To do this, spread bottoms of warm baked macaroons with a little warm, melted apricot jam and sandwich together.

CHOCOLATE MACAROONS

2 eggs
1 cup fine granulated sugar
2½ cups ground unblanched almonds
1½ ounces (squares) bitter chocolate, grated

Beat eggs with sugar until mixture is very thick and almost white. Combine almonds with grated chocolate; add to egg-sugar mixture and mix thoroughly. Drop by teaspoonfuls onto a buttered baking sheet, leaving a 2-inch space between cookies. Bake in preheated 400° oven for 3 minutes. Reduce heat to 350° and bake for about 10 minutes more, or until macaroons are firm enough to retain their shape when pressed and a toothpick inserted in the center comes out clean.

Makes about 1½ dozen cookies

PEPPER NUTS

Whether called Pfeffernüsse in Germany, Pebernødder in Denmark or Pepparnötter in Sweden, these spicy drop cookies are found throughout Northern Europe at Christmas time.

3 eggs
¾ cup dark brown sugar, firmly packed
¾ cup white sugar
Grated rind of 1 lemon
1 tablespoon finely minced citron (optional)
1 tablespoon finely minced candied orange peel (optional)
½ cup grated blanched almonds
2½ cups flour, approximately
1 teaspoon baking powder
1 teaspoon powdered cinnamon
½ teaspoon powdered cloves
½ teaspoon powdered allspice
¼ teaspoon powdered cardamom
½ teaspoon finely ground black pepper
Rum, brandy or arrack
Confectioners' sugar or White Sugar Glaze, page 206

Beat eggs with both sugars until mixture is very thick and almost white. Add lemon rind, fruit, peel, and almonds and mix well. Sift flour with baking powder and spices and stir into egg mixture. Knead on a floured board until smooth. Shape into long rolls about 1 inch in diameter and cut into ½- to ¾-inch slices. Arrange on 3 or 4 large buttered cookie sheets and let dry uncovered in a cool room or refrigerator overnight. Just before baking, turn over each cookie and sprinkle with rum, brandy, or arrack. Bake for about 20 minutes. Roll each cookie in confectioner's sugar while warm, or let cool and ice. These last for weeks if stored in an airtight container.

Makes about 9 dozen cookies

Variation: Any of spices mentioned are optional and to taste. Candied fruits are usually omitted in Scandinavia and 1½ teaspoons powdered ginger is substituted for pepper. In Pennsylvania Dutch country this dough (Pefferniss) is allowed to ripen at room temperature for 1 to 2 weeks, after which it is shaped into rolls, chilled and cut as described. It is then baked without being dried.

NEAPOLITAN MUSTACHES

[*Italy—Mostaccioli*]

½ pound blanched almonds, finely chopped
½ pound walnuts, finely chopped
2 or 3 drops orange-flower water
½ cup honey
1 teaspoon cinnamon
Pinch of freshly ground pepper
2 to 3 egg whites, lightly beaten
1½ cups flour, approximately

Combine nuts, orange water, honey, cinnamon, pepper and enough beaten egg whites to make a paste. Add flour gradually, working in enough to make a thick paste but one that is not too stiff. Spread to ¼- to ½-inch thickness on a board and cut into diamond shapes about 2 inches long. Place on a buttered and floured baking sheet. Bake in preheated 250° oven for 20 to 30 minutes, or until firm.

Makes about 3 dozen cookies

Variation: Follow preceding recipe, but add ¼ cup each chopped citron and candied orange peel. When cookies are baked and cooled, cover with a chocolate icing, pages 203–205.

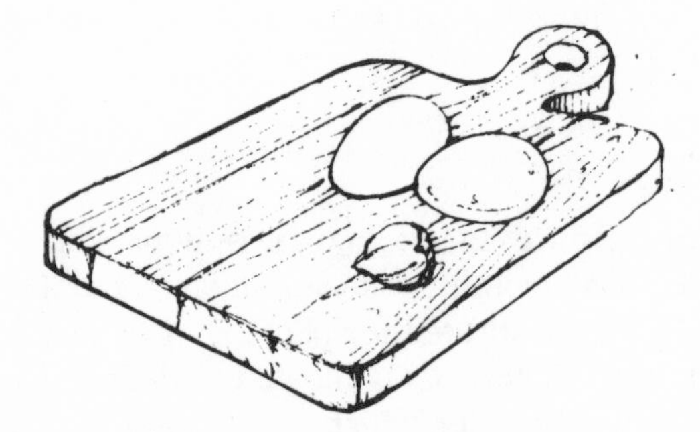

SLAP JACKS

[*Pennsylvania Dutch*]

2½ cups flour
Pinch of salt
½ teaspoon baking soda
1¼ teaspoons baking powder
1¼ cups golden molasses
1¼ cups unsalted butter
1¼ cups sugar
1 cup black walnuts, finely chopped

Sift flour with salt, baking soda and baking powder. Bring molasses to a boil for a minute or two. Stir in butter and sugar until both melt. Remove from heat and resift flour mixture into hot molasses. Fold in walnuts and beat well. Set batter over a pot of hot water. Drop by the teaspoonful, 3 inches apart, on a buttered cookie sheet. Bake in preheated 375° oven for about 8 to 10 minutes. Remove from pan while warm and cool on rack.

Makes about 4½ dozen cookies

SNICKERDOODLES

[*Pennsylvania Dutch and New England*]

½ cup (¼ pound) unsalted butter
¾ cup sugar
1 whole egg
1 egg yolk
1⅔ cups flour
½ teaspoon baking soda
½ teaspoon nutmeg
½ cup coarsely chopped walnuts
½ cup currants or raisins
Nutmeg and sugar, for sprinkling

Cream butter with sugar until light and fluffy. Beat in whole egg and yolk. Sift flour with baking soda and nutmeg. Mix into batter. Fold in nuts and raisins. Drop from a teaspoon 2 inches apart onto buttered cookie sheet. Sprinkle with nutmeg and sugar. Bake in preheated 375° oven for 10 to 12 minutes. Remove from pan while warm. Cool on rack. Store in airtight container.

Makes about 5 dozen cookies

Molded and Shaped Cookies

ALMOND SHELLS

[*Northern Europe*]

- 1 cup (½ pound) unsalted butter
- ¾ cup sugar
- 1¼ cups blanched almonds, finely ground
- 1 teaspoon almond extract
- 1 whole egg
- 1 egg yolk
- 2½ to 3 cups flour
- Whipped cream, jelly or jam

Cream butter with sugar until light and fluffy. Add almonds, extract, egg and yolk to butter and mix thoroughly. Gradually stir in flour until dough is smooth enough to handle. Knead for a minute or two, until smooth, on a lightly floured board. Wrap in waxed paper and chill for 2 hours. Using a generous amount of butter, grease small fluted tart-shell pans. Press an even layer of dough into each pan, making sure that you press it firmly into all the identations. (Keep any leftover dough chilled until you are ready to bake it.) Bake in preheated 375° oven for about 15 minutes, or until a pale golden sand color. Invert over rack and tap bottom of mold gently with a spoon or rub with a cool damp cloth until tart slips out. Cool completely and serve plain or filled with whipped cream and a dab of jam or jelly.

Makes about 5 dozen tarts

BRANDY RING TWISTS

[*Sweden—Konjakskransar*]

1¼ cups unsalted butter
⅔ cup sugar
1 egg yolk
3 tablespoons brandy
3¼ cups flour, approximately
Cinnamon Sugar, page 211, or granulated sugar

Cream butter and sugar until light and fluffy. Beat egg yolk with brandy and mix into creamed butter. Gradually sift in just enough flour to make a smooth but soft dough. Gather this into a ball and chill for 1 to 2 hours. Pinch off small pieces of dough, and on a lightly floured board, roll into thin pencil strips, each about 5 inches long. Twist these rolls together in pairs, rope fashion, and turn into rings. Dough should remain cold until it is rolled, so divide into portions and keep some chilled while you prepare the rest. Sprinkle with sugar of your choice and place on a lightly buttered baking sheet. Bake in preheated 350° oven for about 10 minutes, or until pale golden yellow. Cool and store in airtight container.

Makes about 5 dozen cookies

HAZELNUT CRESCENTS

[*Northern and Central Europe*]

1 cup (½ pound) unsalted butter
⅓ cup sugar
1 cup ground unblanched hazelnuts
1 teaspoon vanilla or cinnamon
2¼ cups flour, sifted
Pinch of salt

Cream butter with sugar until light and fluffy and mix in nuts. Add flavoring. Sift flour with salt and gradually resift into butter mixture, beating well between additions until dough is smooth enough to roll. Break off pieces of dough and press into crescent shapes about 3 inches long. Arrange on a buttered cookie sheet. Bake in preheated 350° oven for about 10 minutes.

Makes about 8 dozen cookies

FINNISH CHESTNUT FINGERS

- ¾ cup unsalted butter
- ⅔ cup sugar
- 4 eggs, well beaten
- ½ teaspoon salt
- ½ teaspoon cinnamon
- 1 teaspoon vanilla
- 1 pound peeled, boiled or roasted fresh or canned chestnuts, ground, or 2 cups unseasoned chestnut purée
- 3 cups flour
- 1 egg white, lightly beaten
- Sugar, for sprinkling
- Ground blanched almonds (optional)

Cream butter and sugar until light and fluffy. Add eggs, one at a time, beating well between additions. Add salt, cinnamon, vanilla and ground chestnuts or chestnut purée, and beat. Sift flour into mixture and blend thoroughly. Roll into 2-inch strips ¾-inch thick and press into finger shapes. Brush with lightly beaten egg white and sprinkle tops with sugar or sugar and ground almonds. Place on a buttered and floured baking sheet. Bake in preheated 350° oven for about 15 minutes, or until a pale sand color.

Makes about 4 dozen cookies

MERINGUES

[*Europe*]

- 4 egg whites
- Pinch of salt
- ¼ teaspoon cream of tartar
- 1 teaspoon vanilla or almond extract or lemon juice
- 1 cup plus 1 tablespoon sugar
- Paper cookie stickers, page 243, colored sugar, page 243, or sugar sprinkles, page 244, or a chocolate icing, pages 203–205

Place 2 cookie sheets in a slow oven until they are slightly warm. Butter lightly, cut a piece of waxed paper to fit each sheet, then spread top of paper with another light coating of butter. Beat egg whites with salt, cream of tartar and flavoring until they begin to hold soft peaks. Gradually add sugar, beating well between additions until all sugar is in and whites are very stiff and dull; a clean cut should remain when a knife blade is passed through. Put into a pastry bag fitted with a wide saw-toothed tube.

Press onto baking sheets in circles, "S" shapes, strips or mounds or peaked kisses, in any sizes you choose. Place in preheated 200° oven (or 175° oven if possible) and let meringues dry completely. This will take between 45 minutes and 1 hour. They should remain absolutely white. Loosen from paper and let them cool in oven with heat off and door open. When cold, store in airtight container. Decorate meringues by placing paper stickers onto bottom of each cookie; or tops can be sprinkled with colored sugar or sprinkles before baking; or spread cooled cookies with icing.

Makes about thirty 2½- to 3-inch circles or "S" forms

SPRITZ COOKIES

[*Germany and Northern Europe*]

1 cup (½ pound) unsalted butter
½ cup sugar
¼ teaspoon salt
1 teaspoon vanilla or almond extract, or grated rind of ½ lemon
2 teaspoons cinnamon (optional)
1 egg
2¼ cups sifted flour, approximately

Let butter soften slightly at room temperature; then cream with sugar and salt until mixture is light and fluffy. Add flavoring and egg and blend thoroughly. Stir in enough flour to make a soft workable dough. Pack dough into cookie press or pastry bag, using any pattern you prefer. Lightly butter baking sheets. Press out dough into rings, strips, or any shape you choose. Bake in preheated 375° oven for about 10 minutes, or until cookie edges are light golden brown.

Makes about 5 dozen cookies

RICCIARELLI DI SIENA

[*Italy*]

½ pound blanched almonds
1 cup granulated sugar
1 cup confectioners' sugar, or as needed
½ teaspoon vanilla extract
2 egg whites, lightly beaten
Bakers' rice wafers, page 242 (optional)
Vanilla Sugar (confectioners'), page 211

Dry blanched almonds in 275° oven for a few minutes. Grind as fine as possible, then place in a mortar and work in granulated sugar until you have a smooth paste. Rub the nut-sugar mixture through a sieve. Mix in 1 cup confectioners' sugar and vanilla. Whisk egg whites until frothy; then mix into nuts. Add additional confectioners' sugar if needed to make a paste dry enough to handle.

If you are using wafers, cut them into ovals 2½ inches long by 1½ inches wide. Spread a level tablespoonful of the almond paste in a ¼- to ½-inch-thick layer on each wafer and place on buttered and floured baking sheets. If you are not using wafers, dust your hands with confectioners' sugar and shape the same size ovals of the almond paste. Place 1 inch apart on oiled brown paper set on a baking sheet. Let dry overnight. Bake in preheated 275° oven for 30 to 40 minutes, or until dry but still white. Sprinkle with vanilla sugar while warm. Cool on a rack, sprinkle with sugar again and store in airtight container.

Makes about 2 dozen cookies

SWEDISH CINNAMON SAND COOKIES

[*Kanelkakor*]

¾ cup unsalted butter
1¼ cups sugar
1 whole egg
1 egg yolk
1 teaspoon cinnamon
1 teaspoon powdered cardamom
1 teaspoon baking powder
1¾ to 2 cups flour
1 egg, lightly beaten
Granulated sugar or coarsely crushed sugar cubes
Cinnamon

Cream butter with sugar until light and fluffy. Beat in egg and egg yolk. Sift spices with baking powder and 1¾ cups flour. Gradually resift into butter mixture, beating well between additions. Add more flour if necessary to make a dough that can be rolled in your hands. Chill 30 minutes. Roll dough between your hands into walnut-size balls. Flatten slightly and brush tops of cookies with beaten egg. Sprinkle with sugar and cinnamon. Place about 3 inches apart on a buttered baking sheet. Bake in preheated 350° oven for about 12 to 15 minutes, or until crisp. If you prefer, dough can be rolled between sheets of waxed paper to ¼-inch thickness and cut with round scalloped cutter, then baked.

Makes about 7 dozen cookies

VANILLA OR BERLIN WREATHS

[*Denmark—Vanillekranser; Germany—Berlinerkranzen*]

1½ cups (¾ pound) unsalted butter
2 cups sugar
2 eggs, lightly beaten
½ cup ground unblanched almonds
1 teaspoon vanilla extract
3½ cups sifted flour

Cream butter with sugar until light and fluffy. Blend in eggs. Add almonds and vanilla and stir well. Gradually add flour, stirring well between additions. Put batter into pastry bag or cookie press. Butter and flour baking sheets and press dough onto them in wreath shapes, each about 2 inches in diameter, using a tube that will give a fluted, ropelike pattern; or roll dough into 6-inch-long pencil strips, twist to ropelike pattern and form a wreath. Bake in preheated 325° oven for 20 to 25 minutes, or until light golden brown.

Makes about 4 dozen cookies.

Variation: To give these cookies a more decorative finish, brush them with a little egg yolk beaten with water, sprinkle with sugar and then bake. Or brush with a mixture of 1 egg white beaten with 1½ tablespoons sugar and dot with candied cherry halves.

VANILLA PRETZELS

[*Denmark—Vanillekringler; Germany—Vanillebrezeln*]

For the significance of the pretzel shape at Christmas, see page 18.

3½ cups flour
1 teaspoon baking powder
1 cup (½ pound) unsalted butter
1 egg, lightly beaten
1 teaspoon vanilla
1 cup sugar
½ cup heavy cream
1 egg, lightly beaten
½ cup finely chopped unblanched almonds
2 or 3 tablespoons sugar

Sift flour with baking powder into a wide bowl. Form a well in flour. To this add butter, cut into small pieces, 1 beaten egg, vanilla, sugar and cream. Work ingredients together with your fingertips until you have a smooth dough that sticks together. Form a ball, wrap in waxed paper and chill 30 minutes. Break dough off in pieces slightly larger than a walnut. With floured hands, roll each piece to a thin rope. Shape into a pretzel. Arrange on buttered baking sheet and chill 20 minutes. Brush with beaten egg and sprinkle with chopped almonds, then sugar. Bake in preheated 325° oven for about 25 minutes, or until golden brown.

Makes about 3 dozen cookies

Variation: The almond and sugar topping may be omitted and the pretzels baked and cooled, then spread with White Sugar Glaze, page 206.

ALMOND SPICE BREAD

[*Belgium—Pain D'Amandes*]

4 cups sifted flour
1 scant teaspoon baking powder
1 teaspoon cinnamon
Pinch of salt
1¾ cups blanched almonds, grated
1 cup plus 2 tablespoons firmly packed light brown sugar
¼ cup brandy
½ cup milk
¾ cup unsalted butter, melted

Sift flour with baking powder, cinnamon and salt. Stir in almonds and sugar. Combine brandy, milk and butter, and stir into flour mixture. Add more flour if necessary to give a dough that will pack together firmly. Press into a roll, wrap in waxed paper and chill overnight. Cut into ½-inch-thick slices. Arrange on a lightly buttered cookie sheet. Bake in preheated 375° oven for 10 minutes. Cool on a rack.

Makes about 5 dozen cookies

VICTORIAN CURRANT CAKES

[*England*]

1 cup currants
½ cup brandy, heated
1 cup plus 2 tablespoons unsalted butter
1 heaping cup sugar
1 whole egg
1 egg yolk
½ teaspoon nutmeg
½ teaspoon cinnamon
2½ to 2¾ cups flour

Soak currants in brandy for 30 minutes; drain and reserve brandy. Cream butter with sugar until light and fluffy. Add egg and yolk with spices and mix well. Add 2 teaspoons reserved brandy and the currants and mix thoroughly. Gradually add enough flour to make a smooth but light dough. Wrap in waxed paper and chill 1 hour. Pinch off small pieces of dough and roll between floured hands to balls about 1 inch in diameter. Arrange on a buttered cookie sheet about 2 inches apart. Flatten each cookie with the tines of a fork. Bake in preheated 350° oven for about 10 minutes, or until pale golden brown.

Makes about 6 dozen cookies

Rolled Cookies

BASELER LECKERLI

[*Switzerland*]

- 1¼ cups honey
- ⅓ cup kirsch
- 1 cup sugar
- ¼ cup diced candied lemon peel
- ¼ cup diced candied orange peel
- Grated rind of 1 lemon
- 1 cup coarsely ground unblanched almonds
- 3 to 3½ cups sifted flour, as needed
- 1 tablespoon cinnamon
- 1 teaspoon nutmeg
- ½ teaspoon powdered cloves
- Pinch of salt
- 1 teaspoon baking soda
- White Sugar Glaze, page 206

Place honey in a large saucepan and bring to a boil. Remove from heat and stir in kirsch and sugar. Place over low heat, stirring constantly until sugar dissolves. Add fruit peel and grated rind and cool to lukewarm. Stir in almonds. Resift 3 cups flour with spices, salt and soda and stir into mixture in pot. Dough should be thick enough to leave the sides of the pan when stirred. Add more flour if necessary.

Cover dough and let ripen in cool corner for 2 days to 1 week. Roll out dough to ½-inch thickness and cut into 2- by 3-inch rectangles, or shape with Leckerli or Springerle molds and cut cookies apart. Arrange cookies close together on well-buttered and floured baking sheet. Bake in preheated 325° oven for 20 to 25 minutes, or until golden brown. Brush with glaze while warm.

Makes about 2½ dozen cookies

BERNER LECKERLI

[*Switzerland*]

- 1/3 cup diced candied orange peel, soaked in kirsch and well drained
- 2½ cups sugar
- ½ cup flour
- 1 teaspoon cinnamon
- 1 tablespoon honey
- 1 cup shelled unblanched almonds, coarsely ground
- 1 cup shelled hazelnuts, coarsely ground
- 5 egg whites, stiffly beaten
- White Sugar Glaze, page 206

Combine all ingredients except egg whites and glaze. After whites are stiffly beaten, stir in gradually until dough is fairly stiff. Chill 5 to 6 hours. Roll out to ½-inch thickness. Shape with floured Leckerli or Springerle molds, cut cookies apart and arrange on a buttered and floured cookie sheet. Bake in preheated 350° oven for 5 to 7 minutes, or until golden brown. Brush hot cookies with glaze. When thoroughly cool, store in airtight container.

Makes about 2½ dozen cookies

BROWN CAKES

[*Denmark—Brunekager*]

- 1 cup (½ pound) unsalted butter
- 1 cup dark corn syrup
- 1 cup brown sugar, firmly packed
- 1 teaspoon baking soda
- ½ teaspoon powdered cardamom
- ½ teaspoon powdered cloves
- 1 teaspoon cinnamon
- ½ teaspoon allspice
- Grated rind of 1 large orange
- 2 tablespoons diced candied orange peel (optional)
- 2 tablespoons diced candied lemon peel (optional)
- ½ teaspoon almond extract, or 1 tablespoon brandy
- 4 to 5 cups flour
- ½ pound blanched almonds, split in half

Combine butter, corn syrup and sugar and heat slowly until all ingredients melt. Remove from heat and stir in baking soda, spices, fruit peel and flavoring. Stir in flour gradually until you have a firm dough that is not sticky. Knead until smooth. Place dough in a bowl, cover with waxed paper and let stand for 2 to 3 weeks in the refrigerator. Roll out until thin and cut into rounds, squares or Christmas shapes. Place half an almond in the center of each cookie. Arrange on buttered baking sheet. Bake in preheated 375° oven for about 10 minutes.

Makes 5 to 6 dozen cookies

BELSNICKLES

[*Pennsylvania Dutch*]

These cookies used to be given to the masked revelers (Belsnickles) who went bell-ringing from one house to another on Christmas Eve.

½ cup (¼ pound) melted unsalted butter
1 cup sugar
1 whole egg
2 egg yolks
1 to 1½ cups flour
½ teaspoon baking soda
Pinch of salt
Granulated sugar, for sprinkling

Pour butter over sugar and beat until creamy. Add eggs and beat well. Sift flour twice with baking soda and salt. Resift gradually into butter mixture, adding only enough flour to make a dough you can roll. Beat thoroughly until mixture holds together. Chill several hours. Roll out to paper thinness on a lightly floured board. Cut into 1-inch rounds, sprinkle liberally with granulated sugar and place on a buttered baking sheet. Bake in preheated 400° oven for 8 to 10 minutes, or until faintly golden around the edges.

Makes 4 to 5 dozen cookies

BELLYLAPS

[*Pennsylvania Dutch*]

These are similar to the Moravian Brown Sugar Cookies, page 115, and a little less brittle, so they can be used for tree ornaments.

2 cups golden molasses
⅓ cup melted unsalted butter
1 egg, well beaten
4 cups flour, approximately
2 teaspoons baking soda
2 teaspoons cinnamon
½ teaspoon nutmeg

Mix molasses with butter and the beaten egg. Sift flour twice with baking soda and spices. Resift into molasses mixture gradually, adding just enough flour to make a dough you can roll. Roll out to ¼-inch thickness on a lightly floured board. Cut with animal and other fancy cookie cutters. These are usually made in fairly large sizes, about 4 inches in width. Place on a buttered and floured baking sheet. Bake in preheated 350° oven for 10 to 15 minutes.

Makes about 3 dozen cookies

CINNAMON STARS

[*Germany—Zimtsterne*]

3 egg whites
1¼ cups fine granulated sugar
3 teaspoons cinnamon
1½ pounds grated unblanched almonds
½ teaspoon almond extract, or 1 teaspoon brandy
Finely ground nuts or fine granulated sugar, for pastry board

Beat egg whites and as they begin to get foamy and stiff gradually beat in sugar. Continue beating until whites form stiff peaks that retain the mark of a knife blade. Set aside ½ cup of whites. Sprinkle remaining whites with cinnamon, 1½ cups almonds and extract or brandy. Stir together gently but thoroughly. Mixture should be thick and fairly solid. Add more almonds if dough is too sticky to be rolled. Sprinkle pastry board with nuts or sugar and roll out dough to ¼-inch thickness. Cut into star shapes with cookie cutter. Arrange on buttered baking sheet and brush top of each cookie with a little of the reserved egg whites. Bake in preheated 300° oven for about 20 minutes, or until golden brown.

Makes about 6 dozen cookies

FINNISH BREAD

[*Finska Pinnar*]

Called either "bread" or "fingers," this cookie is claimed by both Swedes and Finns, and no Danish or Norwegian cookbook would be complete without a recipe for it.

1 cup (½ pound) unsalted butter
½ cup sugar
1 teaspoon vanilla or almond extract
2½ cups flour
2 egg yolks beaten with 2 tablespoons cold water
½ cup finely chopped blanched almonds
Sugar, for sprinkling

Let butter soften slightly at room temperature; then cream with sugar until light and fluffy. Add flavoring and gently mix in flour until just blended, but not too smooth. With lightly floured hands roll dough into long strips about the thickness of a little finger. Cut into 2- to 3-inch lengths and press top lightly with the back of your finger. Brush with beaten egg yolk and sprinkle with almonds and sugar. Place close together on an unbuttered baking sheet. Bake in preheated 375° oven for 10 to 12 minutes, or until golden.

Makes about 3 dozen cookies

SWEDISH GINGERSNAPS

The Swedish name for these cookies, Pepparkakor, is a reminder of the fact that in medieval times ginger and pepper were always used together, and their names became interchangeable. That is why so many ginger-flavored cookies and cakes are called "pepper" though they contain none of that spice but are spicy or "peppery" in flavor.

¾ cup unsalted butter
1 cup firmly packed light brown sugar
2½ tablespoons golden molasses
3 tablespoons boiling water
Grated rind of ½ lemon
2¾ cups sifted flour
1 teaspoon baking soda
2 teaspoons cinnamon
1 teaspoon powdered cloves
1 teaspoon powdered cardamom
1½ teaspoons ginger
Decorative Sugar Icing, page 207

Cream butter with sugar until light and fluffy. Mix molasses with water and add to butter mixture along with lemon rind. Sift flour with baking soda and spices. Add 2½ cups to batter and stir in thoroughly. Add remaining flour if necessary to give a dough smooth enough to roll but one that is still soft and pliable. Knead dough briefly until smooth on a lightly floured board. Wrap in waxed paper and chill for 1 hour. Roll out to paper thinness on lightly floured board. Cut into figures of boys, girls, hearts, stars, circles, etc., with cookie cutters. Arrange on a lightly buttered baking sheet and bake in preheated 350° oven for about 10 minutes. Cool and decorate as shown on page 110.

Makes about 5 dozen 2½-inch cookies

GINGERBREAD MEN

Follow recipe for Swedish Gingersnaps (above). Then, using a cutter, or working from a paper pattern, cut out gingerbread men or women in any sizes you want.

LUCIA GINGERSNAPS

[*Sweden*]

These beautiful blond ginger wafers have a mellow spicy flavor that is unusual. It is one of the easiest doughs to work with that I have ever come across.

- **1½ cups heavy sweet cream**
- **2½ cups brown sugar, firmly packed**
- **¾ cup molasses**
- **½ cup dark corn syrup**
- **1 tablespoon ginger**
- **Grated rind of 1½ lemons**
- **2 tablespoons baking soda**
- **8 to 9 cups flour, as needed**
- **Decorative Sugar Icing, page 207**

Whip cream until almost stiff. Combine sugar, molasses, syrup, ginger, lemon rind and baking soda and mix thoroughly. Pour into cream and beat for 10 minutes by hand, 4 minutes in an electric mixer. Add 5 cups of flour and blend in thoroughly. Beat in remaining flour gradually until dough is just smooth enough to handle but still soft and pliable. Wrap in waxed paper and chill several hours or overnight.

Roll out to ¼-inch thickness on a lightly floured board. Cut into fancy shapes, such as animals, boys, girls, stars, hearts and crescents, with cookie cutters about 2½ inches wide. Place on a lightly buttered cookie sheet and bake in preheated 275° oven for about 12 minutes, or until evenly golden brown. When cool, decorate with icing.

Makes about 5 dozen cookies

GRANDMOTHER'S JELLY COOKIES

[*Sweden—Mormors Syltkakor; Germany—Spitzbuben*]

1 cup (½ pound) unsalted butter
¾ cup sugar
1 egg
3 cups sifted flour
½ teaspoon salt
2 egg whites, lightly beaten
½ cup finely chopped blanched almonds or unblanched walnuts
¼ to ⅓ cup sugar
¼ to ½ cup red currant jelly

Cream butter with sugar until light and fluffy. Beat in egg. Sift flour with salt and resift into butter mixture. Mix thoroughly. Chill for 1 hour. Divide dough in half and roll one portion out to ⅛-inch thickness on a lightly floured board. Cut with round cookie cutter about 2½ inches in diameter. Roll out second portion of dough and cut with scalloped round cookie cutter that is 2 inches in diameter. Using a very small cutter or a thimble, cut a small circle out of the center of the smaller rounds. Brush tops of smaller cookies with lightly beaten egg white and sprinkle with chopped nuts and sugar. Bake all cookies on buttered cookie sheets in preheated 375° oven for 10 to 12 minutes. Cool completely. Place a spoonful of jelly in the center of large cookies. Top with smaller cookies and press together gently.

Makes about 4 dozen cookies

CAVALUCCI DI SIENA

Like the German Springerle, Cavalucci means little horses, referring to the picture originally stamped onto these cookies. They are not usually stamped now, though you can decorate them with a Springerle mold if you like. This recipe is adapted from one that appears in Pelligrino Artusi's nineteenth-century cooking classic *La Scienza in Cucina e l'Arte di Mangiar Bene*—Science in the Kitchen and the Art of Eating Well.

1¾ cups sugar
⅓ cup finely minced candied orange peel
1 heaping tablespoon anise seeds, crushed
1 teaspoon cinnamon
½ cup ground walnuts
2¾ cups flour, approximately

Combine sugar and ½ cup water in a heavy-bottomed saucepan. Bring to a boil and cook rapidly without stirring until mixture forms a thread when a spoon is lifted out of it, or until it reaches 230° on a candy thermometer. Quickly fold in orange peel, anise seeds, cinnamon, ground nuts and enough flour to make a smooth dough. Turn onto a lightly floured board, and when mixture is cool enough to handle, knead until smoothly blended, adding more flour only if necessary. Roll out to ¼- to ½-inch thickness and cut into ovals about 1¾ inches long and 1¼ inches wide. Or stamp design onto rolled-out dough and cut cookies apart.

Place on a buttered and floured cookie sheet. Bake in preheated 275° oven for about 40 to 50 minutes. Cookies should be dry but should not take on color. They will be moist in the center. Store in airtight container.

Makes 4 to 5 dozen, depending on size

MAILÄNDERLI

[*Switzerland*]

In spite of their name, which derives from Milan, these delicious butter cookies are a Swiss Christmas trademark. They are quite typical of rolled and cut butter cookies made at Christmas throughout Europe.

½ cup (¼ pound) unsalted butter
¾ cup sugar
1 egg
2 egg yolks
Grated rind of 1 lemon
Grated rind of ½ orange (optional)
2 tablespoons kirsch or white pear brandy (Birnenschnapps)
2⅔ cups flour, approximately
½ teaspoon salt
1 egg yolk beaten with 1 tablespoon water
Granulated sugar (optional)

Let butter soften slightly at room temperature. Cream with a wooden spoon and gradually blend with sugar until mixture is light and fluffy. Beat whole egg, yolks, grated rind and kirsch and add to butter. Mix well until thoroughly blended. Add 2 cups of flour mixed with salt and stir in. Add remaining flour gradually, blending well between additions until dough is just smooth enough to be handled. Knead quickly for a minute or two until dough is smooth, adding more flour if necessary. Wrap in waxed paper and chill overnight.

Roll out dough to ¼-inch thickness between two sheets of waxed paper. Turn it after each roll and loosen paper every two or three rolls to allow dough to spread. Cut into fancy shapes with cookie cutters that are about 1½ inches in diameter or width. Knead and reroll scraps of dough and cut into shapes. If scraps become sticky, chill until smooth and then roll and cut.

Place cookies ½ inch apart on buttered and floured baking sheets. Brush with egg yolk glaze. Sprinkle with granulated sugar if you like. Bake in preheated 350° oven for 12 to 15 minutes, or until cookies are golden brown around edges and bright gold in the center. Cool completely on a rack. Store in airtight containers.

Makes between 4 and 5 dozen cookies

PORTUGUESE BROASS

Follow preceding recipe, using an extra ½ teaspoon salt and an extra ⅓ cup sugar; use 2 whole eggs and no egg yolks. Sift flour with 1 teaspoon baking powder and add to other ingredients, as described. Knead and chill, then with floured hands roll into balls 1 inch in diameter. Arrange on a buttered cookie sheet. Top with colored sugar, page 243, or sugar sprinkles, page 244. Bake in preheated 375° oven for 10 minutes.

SWISS ALMOND COOKIES

[*Mandel Guestle*]

Follow Mailänderli recipe, using only ½ cup sugar and 2 cups of flour. Add ⅔ cup grated blanched almonds with the flour.

Makes between 4 and 5 dozen cookies

GERMAN NUT SLICES

[*Nussplatzchen*]

Follow recipe for Portuguese Broass (above). Chill for 30 minutes and roll out to ⅛-inch thickness. Cut with a 1½- to 2½-inch round cookie cutter. Place on a buttered baking sheet. Chill 30 minutes. Brush tops of cookies with 1 beaten egg and sprinkle with chopped hazelnuts or almonds and granulated sugar. Bake at 350° for 8 to 10 minutes.

MORAVIAN BROWN SUGAR COOKIES

[*Pennsylvania Dutch*]

These cookies are usually served to visitors who come to see the family Christmas crèche.

- 1 cup (½ pound) unsalted butter
- 2 cups sugar
- ¼ cup light sweet cream
- 2 cups black molasses
- 2 tablespoons cinnamon
- 1 tablespoon ginger
- 1 teaspoon powdered cloves
- ½ teaspoon nutmeg
- 7 to 8 cups flour, approximately

Cream butter with sugar until light and fluffy. Beat in cream, molasses and spices. Sift flour in gradually, beating well between additions, until you have a stiff dough that can be rolled. Roll out to paper thinness on lightly floured board and cut into fancy shapes with cookie cutters about 1½ to 2 inches wide. Place cookies on buttered and floured baking sheet and bake in preheated 350° oven for 10 to 12 minutes, or until a mellow brown color but not darkened around edges. Slide onto a rack, cool and store in airtight container.

Makes about 8 dozen cookies

Variation: If you do not like a strong molasses flavor, use golden molasses instead of the black, or use a half-and-half combination of molasses and golden corn syrup. For a richer flavor, let dough stand in a cool place (not in the refrigerator) 5 or 6 hours or overnight before rolling and cutting.

POLISH HONEY KISSES

[*Ciastka Miodowe*]

Follow preceding recipe, using honey instead of molasses. Add the grated rind of 1 lemon. Decorate with Decorative Sugar Icing, page 207. These are used as Christmas tree ornaments.

MORAVIAN WHITE SUGAR COOKIES

[*Pennsylvania Dutch*]

- 4 cups flour
- 1 scant teaspoon cinnamon
- ½ teaspoon nutmeg
- 1 cup (½ pound) unsalted butter
- 2¼ cups sugar
- 4 eggs, well beaten
- 2 tablespoons sherry, brandy or rum

Sift flour with spices and set aside. Cream butter with sugar until light and fluffy. Add well-beaten eggs and sherry, brandy or rum to the butter mixture and beat in until smoothly blended. Gradually resift flour into mixture, beating well between additions. Roll out to paper thinness on lightly floured board and cut into fancy shapes with 2-inch cookie cutters. Place on buttered baking sheet. Bake in preheated 350° oven for about 10 to 12 minutes, or until crisp and a pale sand color. Cool on a rack and store in an airtight container.

Makes about 4 dozen cookies

Note: This dough can be allowed to mellow in a cool place (not the refrigerator) 5 to 6 hours or overnight before being rolled and cut.

PASTINI DI NATALE

[*Italy*]

- ½ teaspoon salt
- 2 teaspoons baking powder
- 3 cups flour
- 1 cup (½ pound) unsalted butter
- 1¼ cups sugar
- 1 whole egg
- 2 egg yolks
- 1 tablespoon rum
- 1 tablespoon lemon juice
- Grated rind of 1 lemon
- ⅓ cup minced pine nuts or unsalted pistachios

Sift salt, baking powder and flour together into a wide bowl. Using two knives or a pastry blender, cut in butter until mixture resembles coarse meal. Beat sugar with whole egg, yolks and lemon rind, juice and rum. Add with nuts to flour mixture. Mix until dough is firm. Knead lightly for 1 or 2 minutes, wrap in waxed paper and chill for 1 hour. Divide dough in half and roll each half out to ¼-inch thickness. Cut into Christmas shapes with cookie cutters. Arrange on unbuttered baking sheets and bake in preheated 425° oven for 10 minutes, or until light golden brown. Cool completely and decorate with colored icing.

Makes about 3 dozen cookies

Variation: This dough is often tinted with a few drops of food coloring. If you like, you can brush the shaped cookies with egg yolk beaten with 1 tablespoon water, then sprinkle with colored sugar, page 243, or sugar sprinkles, page 244, before baking.

SPECULATIONS

The biggest speculation about these cookies concerns their origin. They are claimed by the Dutch, the Danish, the Belgians and the Rhinelanders. They are also Christmas standards in our own Pennsylvania Dutch country. In Holland, windmill-patterned Speckulaas molds are pressed onto the rolled-out dough, while in other countries, Santa Claus, Christmas trees, stars and wreaths are used. Springerle forms can be substituted for Speckulaas molds.

- 1 cup (½ pound) unsalted butter
- 2 cups brown sugar, firmly packed
- Grated rind of ½ lemon
- 2 eggs
- ½ teaspoon powdered cloves or ⅛ teaspoon powdered cardamom
- 1 tablespoon cinnamon
- 1 teaspoon nutmeg
- 4 cups flour, sifted
- 1 teaspoon baking powder
- 2 to 3 tablespoons milk, or as needed
- ¼ cup blanched chopped almonds (optional)

Let butter soften slightly at room temperature. Then cream with sugar until fluffy. Add lemon rind and mix in eggs. Beat in spices.

Resift flour with baking powder and stir into butter mixture. Add milk as needed to make dough smooth. Knead dough gently, adding almonds. Chill 4 to 5 hours. Roll out to ⅛-inch thickness and press patterns in with floured mold. Cut cookies apart and place on lightly buttered baking sheets. (Scraps of dough can be gathered together, rolled, chilled and reshaped.) Bake in preheated 400° oven for 8 minutes. Reduce heat to 325° and bake 25 minutes more, or until golden brown.

Makes about 3½ dozen cookies

SWEDISH UPPÄKRA COOKIES

[*Uppakrakakor*]

1 cup (½ pound) unsalted butter
½ cup confectioners' sugar, sifted
⅔ cup potato flour or starch
1⅔ cup flour
1 egg, lightly beaten
½ cup chopped blanched almonds
3 tablespoons sugar

Cream butter with confectioners' sugar until light and fluffy. Sift flours together and resift into butter, blending thoroughly. Knead for a minute or two. Chill dough for 30 minutes. Dough should remain chilled until it is to be rolled, so divide into quarters and leave pieces in refrigerator until you are ready for them. Roll out between sheets of waxed paper to paper thinness. Cut with 2-inch round cookie cutter. Fold each cookie almost in half so that edges do not quite meet. Brush tops with beaten egg and sprinkle with nuts and sugar. Lift carefully with a spatula and place on a buttered cookie sheet. Bake in preheated 350° oven for about 10 minutes, or until pale golden yellow.

Makes about 4 dozen cookies

SPRINGERLE

[*Germany*]

These embossed anise-scented cookies date back to the midwinter pagan celebration, Julfest, during which Germanic tribes sacrificed animals to their gods. The poor, unable to afford the slaughter of their animals, offered token sacrifices of animal-shaped cookies. The name Springerle is derived from the German for a vaulting horse, the sacred animal of Wotan, king of the Nordic gods. In Christian times the Reitersmann—a man riding a horse—became one of the most popular forms to ornament these cookie molds. An outstanding collection of Reitersmann Springerle molds, dating back to the 1500s, can be seen in the Württembergische Landesmuseum, Stuttgart, Germany. See also Cavalucci di Siena, page 112.

4 eggs
2½ cups fine granulated sugar
Grated rind of 1 lemon
5½ cups flour, or as needed
¾ cup lightly crushed anise seeds

Beat eggs and sugar together until mixture is very thick and almost white. Add lemon rind. Sift flour in gradually, beating well between additions. Dough should be smooth enough to knead without sticking to your hands. Add more flour if necessary. Knead dough on floured board until smooth and shiny. With a floured rolling pin, roll dough to a rectangle of ¼- to ½-inch thickness. Flour a Springerle roller, board or individual mold and press or roll design onto dough. Cut cookies apart. Butter a jelly-roll pan or a baking sheet and sprinkle liberally with anise seeds. Place cookies on pan, printed side up, and let dry uncovered, at room temperature, overnight. Bake in preheated 300° oven for about 15 minutes, or until very pale tan. Store in an air-tight box or tin with a piece of apple or bread to prevent hardening (replace apple at frequent intervals).

Makes about 6 dozen cookies

SUGAR DROPS

[*Germany—Zuckerplätzchen*]

⅔ cup unsalted butter
⅔ cup sugar
1 egg yolk
½ teaspoon vanilla extract
4 tablespoons light sweet cream
Grated rind of ½ lemon
1⅔ cups flour
½ teaspoon baking powder
Pinch of salt
½ cup finely minced candied fruit peel
1 recipe Meringue Snow Frosting, page 209
Candied cherries

Cream butter with sugar until light and fluffy. Beat in egg yolk, vanilla, cream and lemon rind. Sift flour with baking powder and salt and resift gradually into butter mixture, beating well between additions. Add more flour if needed to make a dough that can be gathered into a ball, but is not too stiff. Mix in the candied fruit peel. Chill dough for 2 hours; then roll out to a little less than ¼-inch thickness. Cut in 1½- to 2-inch rounds with a cookie cutter. Place on buttered baking sheet and top each cookie with 1 teaspoon frosting and a candied cherry. Bake in preheated 350° oven for about 12 minutes, or until cookies are pale golden and crisp and topping is dry but not brown.

Makes about 5 dozen cookies

SWEDISH RYE COOKIES

[*Ragkakor*]

1¼ cups unsalted butter
⅔ cup sugar
1⅓ cups rye flour
1⅓ cups wheat flour
Pinch of salt

Cream butter with sugar until light and fluffy. Sift flours together with salt and add gradually to butter, blending well between additions. Wrap in waxed paper and chill 1 hour. Divide dough in four parts and roll out one at a time, leaving other pieces in the refrigerator until you are ready for them. Roll out to paper thinness on a lightly floured board and cut with 2½-inch round cookie cutters. Arrange on buttered cookie sheets. Using a thimble, cut a small hole off to one side of each cookie. Prick surface of cookies with the tines of a fork. Bake in preheated 350° oven for about 10 minutes, or until golden yellow. Cool on sheet and store in airtight container.

Makes about 5 dozen cookies

STAGS' ANTLERS

[*Scandinavia, especially Finland and Norway*]

¼ cup unsalted butter
¾ cup sugar
2 egg yolks
1 whole egg
¼ cup heavy sweet cream
1 teaspoon powdered cardamom
½ teaspoon salt
½ teaspoon cinnamon (optional)
2 cups flour
1 teaspoon baking soda
¾ cup cornstarch

Cream butter with sugar until light and fluffy. Beat in egg yolks and whole egg. Add cream, cardamom, salt and cinnamon. Sift flour with baking soda and cornstarch and resift into butter mixture. Blend thoroughly. Roll dough out on lightly floured board to ¼-inch thickness. Cut into strips 2 inches long by 1 inch wide. Make two slits on each strip, ¾ inch in from each end, cutting across a little more than half the width of the strip. Curve to open slits. Place on a buttered baking sheet. Bake in preheated 350° oven for about 15 minutes, or until pale golden brown. For extra sweetness additional sugar may be sprinkled on these cookies before baking. Cool on rack and store in airtight container.

Makes about 4 dozen cookies

TIRGGEL COOKIES

[*Switzerland*]

These specialties are always purchased in bakeries, most especially in Zurich, where they originated. Here, they are available in gourmet food shops. They are thin, golden honeyed cookies stamped with Christmas scenes and symbols. They range in size from 2 or 3 inches to 18 inches. The dough, which is relatively tasteless, is said to be very tricky to make. I have not been able to find a recipe for it, and any Swiss bakers I asked merely laughed and said no one ever makes Tirggel at home. If you do, I'd love to have the recipe.

Small Cakes

SCOTS SHORTBREAD

A traditional Christmas and New Year's or Hogmanay treat in Scotland, this crisp butter cake is a direct descendant of the oatmeal bannock served at pagan Yule celebrations. The bannock was a round cake with a circle in the center and ridges around the rim symbolizing the sun and its rays. This decoration is still used for shortbread, which can be made in special wooden molds or as described here. It is considered unlucky to cut this with a knife. Superstition has it that shortbread should be broken into portions.

1½ cups (¾ pound) unsalted butter
1¼ cups confectioners' sugar
3½ cups flour
½ cup rice flour or cornstarch

Cream butter with sugar until light and fluffy. Sift flour with rice flour or cornstarch (the former is preferable if available), and cut into butter until it resembles coarse meal; mix as you would for pastry. Add just enough of the flour mixture to make a dough that can be gathered into a soft ball. Knead on a lightly floured board for a minute or two, only until smooth. Do not knead too long or dough will become greasy and the shortbread will be tough.

Divide dough in half and press each portion into an unbuttered 8-inch layer-cake pan. Using the back of the bowl of a wooden spoon, press a round indentation into the center of the cake and crimp the edges. With the tines of a fork, prick cake all over, right down to the pan. Bake in preheated 350° oven for 45 minutes to 1 hour, or until shortbread is an even pale golden brown.

This will be soft when removed from the oven and can then be cut into wedge-shaped portions; or break when cold and crisp.

Makes two 8-inch cakes

Variation: If you have the wooden shortbread molds, dust them with cornstarch or rice flour, press dough into them and invert onto a buttered and floured cookie sheet.

CHRISTMAS STARS

[*Scandinavia—Julstjärnor*]

FLAKY BUTTER PASTRY:

2½ cups flour
⅔ cup cold unsalted butter
⅓ to ½ cup ice water, approximately

FILLING:

¼ to ½ cup prune jam (lekvar)

TOPPING:

2 egg whites beaten with 2 teaspoons water
Sugar
½ to ⅔ cup grated unblanched almonds (optional)

Sift flour into a wide bowl. Cut cold butter into flour with two knives or a pastry blender until you have granules the size of small peas. Add ice water gradually, tossing mixture together lightly with a fork. Add only enough water to enable dough to stick together in a mass. With floured hands, form a ball, handling the dough as little as possible. Wrap in waxed paper and chill for about 25 minutes.

Turn dough onto a floured board and roll to a rectangle of about ¼-inch thickness. Fold dough lengthwise in thirds. To do this, fold one third of the dough over the center. Fold the remaining third on top, forming three layers. Roll lightly, turn dough over and roll to a rectangle again. Repeat folding and rolling twice more. Wrap in waxed paper and chill again for 25 minutes.

Roll chilled dough out, fold in thirds again and roll into rectangle, making dough a little less than ⅛ inch thick. Trim edges and cut into 4-inch squares. Place squares on lightly buttered baking sheet.

Brush top of each square with beaten egg white and sprinkle liberally with sugar, being careful not to get egg white or sugar too close to edge of cookie squares. Cut a 1½-inch slant from each point toward the center of cookie.

Place a level teaspoonful of jam in the center of the cookie. Fold alternate corners into the center. Brush with egg white. Sprinkle sugar onto corners that were folded over. Sprinkle with almonds and bake in preheated 450° oven for about 7 minutes, or until cookies are light golden brown. (Since these are best when still warm, it is a good idea to bake them shortly before or just after guests arrive. Arrange cookies on baking sheets and keep in refrigerator until you are ready to bake them.) Remove finished cookies from pan carefully with a wide spatula and serve with forks, as this is a very short and fragile dough. Leftover scraps of dough can be pressed together, chilled slightly and rerolled into smaller cookies or pastries.

Makes about a dozen stars

Variation. To make Christmas roses, follow above recipe and place 4-inch squares on baking sheet. Make two 1½-inch diagonal slashes toward center on each side of each corner, so that you have 8 sections. Place a teaspoonful of jam in the center of each cookie. Roll corner tabs toward center. Brush rolls with egg white, sprinkle with sugar, and bake.

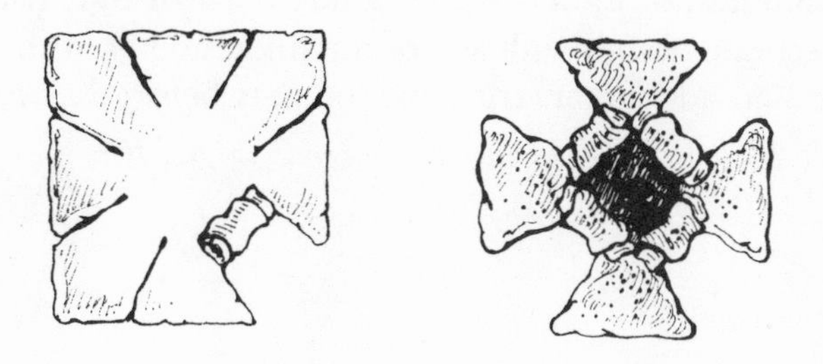

DUTCH ST. NICHOLAS' EVE LETTERS

[*Letterbanket*]

Dutch children leave wooden shoes at the fireplace to be filled by Sinterklaas on December 6th, St. Nicholas' Eve. Those who have been good will find, among other presents, chocolate candy or these almond-filled cakes in the shape of their first initial. These usually range from 2 or 3 inches to 8 inches in height.

- **1 cup (½ pound) unsalted butter or lard**
- **2 cups flour**
- **¼ cup ice water, approximately**
- **2 cups marzipan, purchased or homemade, page 165**
- **1 egg yolk beaten with 2 tablespoons water**
- **Plain or colored sugar, candied cherries and fruit peels, nut meats (optional)**

Cut shortening into flour, using two knives or a pastry blender, until mixture resembles coarse meal. Add ice water, a tablespoon at a time, until dough can be gathered into a ball. Wrap in waxed paper and let stand 30 minutes. Roll out to ¼-inch thickness on a lightly floured board. Cut into strips about 2½ inches wide and 4 inches long. (Vary this for smaller or larger letters.) Roll marzipan into sausage rolls, about 1 inch in diameter. Place these on the strips of dough and close dough over filling, sealing edges with water. Flip over gently so seam is on bottom. Carefully bend into letters. Place on a buttered baking sheet.

Brush with egg yolk glaze and bake in preheated 400° oven for 20 to 30 minutes, or until dough is golden brown and crisp. If you want to decorate dough with any of the suggested garnishes, brush with glaze and add sugar, fruit and/or nuts before baking.

Makes 10 letters 1 to 3 inches tall, or 2 large letters

FRITTERS, DOUGHNUTS & CRULLERS

Chapter Four

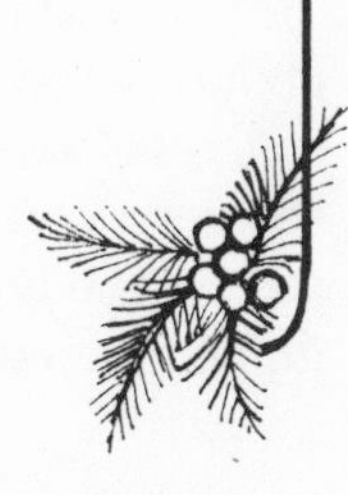

CHOCOLATE CHESTNUT FRITTERS

[*Italy*]

These Calcionetti, or "little kicks," are also called Fritti della Vigilia di Natale—fritters of the Christmas Vigil, which is Christmas Eve. They are a specialty of the Abruzzi.

PASTRY:

2½ cups sifted flour
1 teaspoon salt
1½ tablespoons sugar (optional)
5 tablespoons olive oil or other vegetable oil
⅓ cup white wine, approximately

FILLING:

1 cup cooked unseasoned chestnut purée (½ pound cooked canned chestnuts, drained)
¼ cup chopped toasted blanched almonds or pine nuts
1 ounce (square) semisweet chocolate, grated
2 teaspoons strongly brewed black coffee
1 tablespoon rum, or to taste
Grated rind of 1 orange
2 teaspoons sugar

Oil or vegetable shortening, for deep frying
Vanilla Sugar (confectioners'), page 211

Resift flour with salt and sugar and sprinkle with oil. Toss with a fork or rub flour between your hands until oil is well distributed and mixture resembles a coarse sandy meal. Sprinkle with just enough white wine to enable you to gather the dough into a smooth ball. Wrap in waxed paper and let rest for 15 minutes. Combine all filling ingredients and blend thoroughly.

Divide dough in half and roll each half into a rectangle of about ⅛-inch thickness. Cut each sheet of dough into 2-inch squares. Place a teaspoonful of filling in the center of half of the squares. Wet edges with water and cover with unfilled squares, pinching edges closed and sealing them with the tines of a fork dipped in water. If you prefer, you can prepare this as you would ravioli. Roll out two sheets of dough, as described above, and place teaspoonfuls of filling at 2-inch intervals on one sheet. Cover with unfilled sheet of dough and cut between squares with a ravioli cutter or roller. Seal as above. Heat fat to 375° degrees and fry fritters a few at a time, turning once so both sides become golden brown. Allow about 4 minutes for frying each batch. Drain on paper towel, sprinkle with vanilla sugar and serve warm.

Makes about 2 dozen fritters

ALMOND EMPANADITAS

[*Latin America and the Philippines—Empanaditas de Almendras*]

1 recipe Chocolate Chestnut Fritters pastry, page 128
¾ cup chopped blanched almonds
½ cup sugar
1 teaspoon cinnamon or vanilla
1 egg white
¼ teaspoon almond extract
Oil or vegetable shortening, for deep frying
Cinnamon Sugar, page 211, or Honey Syrup Glaze, page 209

Prepare dough and let rest for 15 minutes. Meanwhile, prepare filling. Mix chopped almonds with sugar and cinnamon or vanilla. Beat egg white with almond extract until frothy and turn through nut mixture. Divide dough in half and roll each portion out to ⅛-inch thickness. The shape is not important. Cut into 2½-inch circles, using a round cookie cutter. Place 1 teaspoonful filling on one half of each circle. Wet edges and fold unfilled half of circle over to form a semicircle. Pinch edges closed, fold over and press closed with the wet tines of a fork.

Heat fat to 375° and fry a few at a time, turning once so both sides become golden brown. Allow about 4 minutes for frying each batch. Drain on a paper towel and sprinkle with cinnamon sugar or drizzle with the glaze while warm.

Makes about 2 dozen empanaditas

DUTCH APPLE FRITTERS

[*Appelbeignets*]

Served on December 6th, St. Nicholas' Eve.

6 to 8 firm, tart apples
2 cups beer
2 cups flour
Pinch of salt
Oil or vegetable shortening, for deep frying
Vanilla Sugar (granulated), page 211

Peel and core apples and cut into lengthwise slices between ⅓ and ½ inch thick. Mix beer with flour and salt until smooth and free of lumps. Dip apple slices into batter and let excess drip off. Fry a few slices at a time in fat heated to 370°. Turn once so they become golden brown on both sides—about 4 minutes in all. Drain on a paper towel and serve warm sprinkled with sugar.

Makes 6 to 10 servings

DREAMS

[*Portugal and Brazil—Sonhos*]

1 cup water
Pinch of salt
½ cup (¼ pound) unsalted butter
1 tablespoon sugar
1 cup flour
4 eggs
Deep fat, for frying
Cinnamon Sugar, page 211, or Honey Syrup Glaze, page 209

Combine water, salt, butter and sugar in a heavy-bottomed 1-quart saucepan. Bring to a boil and simmer until butter melts. Sift flour into liquid. Stir and cook over low heat until mixture forms a mass and leaves the sides of the pan. Remove from heat and beat in eggs, one at a time, blending each thoroughly before adding the next. Continue beating until mixture is shiny. Drop by tablespoons into deep fat heated to 370°. Stir fat frequently with a wooden spoon to keep puffs frying evenly. When golden brown, remove with slotted spoon and drain on paper toweling. Keep finished puffs warm in a slow oven until all are fried. Sprinkle with cinnamon sugar and serve warm. If you like, these can also be served with the honey glaze, flavored with a little orange liqueur.

Makes about 24 puffs

LADIES' THIGHS

[*Switzerland and Alsace*]

Called Schenkele (Shanks) in the German-speaking part of Switzerland and in Alsace, and Cuisses des Dames (Ladies' Thighs) in the French-speaking part of Switzerland, these deep-fried cookies keep for months and are excellent with wine, coffee or frozen desserts. The recipe below was generously given to me by George Schlatter, via his daughter, Suzette, who typed the manuscript for this book.

½ cup (¼ pound) unsalted butter
1 cup sugar
3 eggs
1½ teaspoons almond extract
1½ teaspoons vanilla extract
1 tablespoon kirsch
Grated rind of 1 lemon
1 cup finely chopped walnuts or blanched almonds
½ teaspoon baking powder
½ teaspoon salt
3½ to 4½ cups flour, as needed
Vegetable shortening, for deep frying
Confectioners' sugar (optional)

Cream butter with sugar until light and fluffy. Add eggs, one at a time, beating well between additions. Beat in almond and vanilla extracts, kirsch, lemon rind, nuts, baking powder and salt and beat thoroughly. Gradually sift in flour, beating between additions, until batter is too thick to stir.

Turn out of bowl and knead in as much additional flour as necessary to make a dough that is smooth but pliable. Pinch off pieces of dough, each about the size of a small walnut. Roll, between floured hands, to a cigar (or shank) shape, about 3 inches long and ½ inch at the widest point in the middle, tapering down toward both ends. Place on a platter or board covered with floured waxed paper. Set uncovered in a cool place (not the refrigerator) overnight. Fry a few at a time in deep fat heated to 365° for about

8 minutes, or until golden brown. Drain on a paper towel.

When all are fried and cooled, store in covered tin box in which you have punched a few holes. The flavor of these cookies improves enormously after 24 hours and many people swear they are better yet after a week, if they are not all eaten long before then. They may be sprinkled with confectioners' sugar just before serving.

Makes about 6 to 7 dozen cookies

Variation: Prepare dough and roll out to between ¼ and ½ inch thickness with a floured rolling pin. Cut in cigar shapes, as described, or cut with fancy cookie cutters. Let stand overnight and bake in 375° oven for about 12 to 15 minutes. Cookies may be brushed with egg white and honey before being baked and can be hung on the Christmas tree.

LEBANESE CRULLERS

Known as "zalabiya" when in stick shapes, or "awwamaat" in dumpling shapes, these crullers are served in Lebanon and Syria during the Christmas season and most especially on Ghtas, January 1st, which commemorates Christ's circumcision. It is said that on that day trees kneel in prayer for the Holy Infant.

1 cup yogurt
¼ teaspoon baking soda
Pinch of salt
1¾ cups flour, approximately
Sesame oil or vegetable shortening, for deep frying
Honey Syrup Glaze, page 209, or the sugar syrup below

Beat yogurt until smooth and thin. Mix with baking soda and salt. Sift flour in gradually until mixture can barely be dropped from a spoon. Heat oil to 375°. Using two wet teaspoons, drop spoonfuls of dough, a few at a time, into hot fat. Or wet hands and shape pieces of dough into 2- or 3-inch sticks and drop into fat. Turn once so both sides become golden brown. Allow about 5 minutes for frying each batch. Drain on paper towel and serve with syrup of your choice.

Makes about 2 dozen crullers

Sugar Syrup To make sugar syrup, combine 1 cup sugar and ½ cup water and boil until syrup begins to caramelize and is thin and golden. Skim foam as it rises to surface. Flavor with a few drops of orange-flower water, rose water or lemon juice and pour hot over crullers.

Variation: To make a slightly more solid cruller, sift in enough extra flour to make a dough just smooth enough to knead. Knead for 2 or 3 minutes. Pinch off pieces slightly smaller than walnuts, roll between floured hands, and fry. Vanilla sugar (confectioners'), page 211, though not authentic, is a good substitute for syrup on these crullers, if you prefer them less sweet and sticky.

GREEK DIPLES

"Diples" means "folds" in Greek and refers to the diapers or swaddling clothes of the Christ Child.

1 recipe Smalls or Beggarmen, page 134, made with grated orange rind instead of lemon
Sesame or corn oil, for deep frying
Honey Syrup Glaze, page 209
1 cup chopped walnuts or pistachio nuts, or ½ cup toasted sesame seeds
Vanilla Sugar (confectioners'), page 211

Prepare dough; let rest, as described, then roll out to paper thinness. Using a pastry cutter, cut into 1½-inch squares. Fold these in half diagonally to form triangles, then press touching corners together firmly. Fry a few at a time in oil heated to 375°. Turn once so both sides become golden brown, allowing about 4 minutes for the complete frying of each batch. Drain on a paper towel. When all of the Diples are fried, arrange them in a single layer on a large platter. Cover with hot syrup and sprinkle with chopped nuts or sesame seeds. Cool and sprinkle with sugar before serving.

Makes about 4 dozen

SMALLS OR BEGGARMEN

[*Scandinavia*]

The first name is the translation of the Swedish "Klenäter" and the Danish "Klejner"; the second is from the Norwegian "Fattigmann." In Poland these are called "Chrust."

2 whole eggs
2 egg yolks
1 cup sugar
½ teaspoon salt
¼ cup sweet cream
½ cup (¼ pound) unsalted butter, melted
1 teaspoon baking powder
Grated rind of ½ lemon
1 teaspoon almond or vanilla extract, or ½ teaspoon powdered cardamom
3½ cups flour, approximately
Corn oil or vegetable shortening, for deep frying
Vanilla Sugar (confectioners'), page 211

Beat eggs and yolks with sugar, salt, sweet cream, melted butter, baking powder, lemon rind and flavoring. Sift flour in gradually, stirring between additions until dough is smooth enough to roll. Knead for 1 or 2 minutes and let dough rest in a cool place for ½ hour. Roll out to ¼-inch thickness. Using a pastry cutter, cut strips 1 inch wide by 4 inches long. Cut a 2-inch slit lengthwise in the center of each strip, as shown. Pull one end of strip through the slit to form a half-knot. Fry in oil heated to 375° for about 3 minutes, turning once so they become golden on both sides. Drain on a paper towel. Sprinkle with vanilla sugar.

Makes 4 to 5 dozen crullers

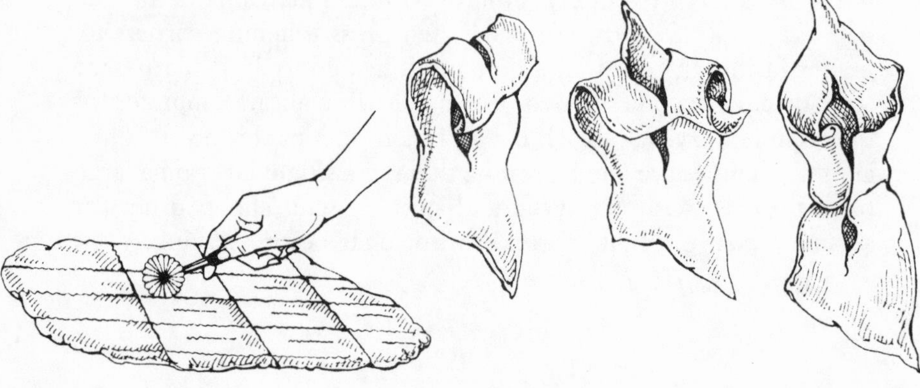

MEXICAN DOUGHNUTS

[*Buñuelos*]

Served all during the Christmas season, these plump fritters or doughnuts are the big feature of the celebration on December 17th honoring Oaxaca's patron saint, the Virgin of Solitude (Virgen de la Soledad). Customers buy the plate in which these are served, and smash it on the ground after they have eaten the cake.

PASTRY:

¾ cup milk, approximately
2 tablespoons anise seeds, lightly crushed
2 eggs, beaten
¼ cup melted unsalted butter
4 cups sifted flour
1 teaspoon baking powder
1 teaspoon salt
Oil, lard or vegetable shortening, for deep frying

SYRUP:

2½ cups dark brown sugar
1 cup water
1 tablespoon anise seeds, lightly crushed, or 1 stick cinnamon

Scald milk with crushed anise seeds and let cool. Beat in eggs and melted butter. Resift flour with baking powder and salt. Combine liquid and dry ingredients and mix well. Add more flour if dough is too sticky, or a little extra unseasoned milk if dough is too crumbly. Knead dough on a floured board for about 10 minutes or until completely smooth.

Divide dough into about 20 pieces and shape into balls the size of lemons. Cover with a towel and press down gently to flatten balls slightly. Let them stand, covered, for about 5 minutes. Fry a few at a time in oil heated to 385°. Turn once so both sides become golden brown. Drain on absorbent paper, break into fork-size pieces and place in individual deep saucers. Boil sugar, water and anise seeds or cinnamon for about 20 minutes, or until the mixture becomes a thick syrup. Strain and pour hot over Buñuelos.

Makes 20 doughnuts

PENNSYLVANIA DUTCH CHRISTMAS DOUGHNUTS

Follow preceding recipe, adding ¾ cup sugar and 1 teaspoon nutmeg and 1 extra teaspoon baking powder to dry ingredients. Eliminate anise seeds. It is not necessary to scald milk. Dredge finished doughnuts with Vanilla Sugar (confectioners'), page 211, or Cinnamon Sugar, page 211. To make lighter doughnuts, add egg yolks to milk and fold in stiffly beaten whites after all other ingredients are combined.

PORTUGUESE CHRISTMAS LOG

[*Nogados*]

Nogados (literally nougat), a golden log of crisply fried pastry strips, is a Christmas dessert from Evora, Portugal.

½ recipe Pignolata dough, page 138
Flour, as needed
Corn oil, for deep frying
Honey Syrup Glaze, page 209, cooked to hard-ball stage (255° on candy thermometer)

Prepare dough, but add a little extra flour to make it firm enough to roll. Roll out to paper thinness and cut into long, thin strips about ¼ inch wide and 3 inches long. Fry a few at a time in oil heated to 375°. Remove with a slotted spoon and drain on a paper towel. When all the strips have been fried, cover them with half the syrup glaze and turn through gently until all are coated. Shape into a log about 10 inches long and 2 to 3 inches wide. Pour remaining syrup glaze over top and sides.

STRUFFOLI

[*Italy*]

This bright pyramid of golden puffs of dough, dripping with honey and festive with sugar confetti, is a specialty of Naples.

4 to 5 cups flour, as needed
1 teaspoon baking powder
½ teaspoon salt
2 eggs
1 egg yolk
1 cup sugar
½ cup (¼ pound) unsalted butter or lard, softened and cut into small pieces
Grated rind of 1 lemon
Corn oil, for deep frying
Honey Syrup Glaze, page 209
Confectioners' sugar, diced candied orange peel and citron, sugar sprinkles

Sift 4 cups of flour with baking powder and salt onto a pastry board or into a wide bowl. Make a well in the center. Beat whole eggs and yolk with sugar, butter and lemon rind and pour into well. Working with your fingertips, quickly blend flour into wet ingredients, adding more if necessary to give a smooth dough that is still soft and pliable. Cover dough with waxed paper and let rest 2 hours. Roll dough out to ½-inch thickness. Cut into strips as wide as your little finger and cut each of these strips into small nutlike pieces, about ½-inch long.

Fry about 30 pieces at a time in corn oil heated to 375°. Remove with a skimmer and drain on a paper towel. Prepare syrup. Add fried puffs to syrup and turn through gently until well coated. Remove with a skimmer and pile onto a serving platter, pressing into a pyramid shape with wet hands. Pour a little honey glaze over the top and sides. Decorate with candied orange peel and citron and sugar sprinkles, then sprinkle with confectioners' sugar. This keeps for a week in the refrigerator. It can be reshaped and decorated, as needed.

PIGNOLATA

[*Italy*]

A rich chocolate-covered version of preceding recipe, this is prepared in the same way, using 2½ cups flour, 4 whole eggs plus 1 yolk, ¼ cup lard and 1 tablespoon sugar. Baking powder is omitted. Mix dough but do not rest or roll it. Pull off pieces about the size of small walnuts, and fry. Dip each puff into Creamy Chocolate Icing, page 205, and pile in a tall mound. Pour remaining icing over top and let it drip down the sides.

CROCCANTE DI NATALE

To make the Sicilian version of Struffoli, prepare and fry dough as described in basic recipe, page 137. As fried nuggets are turned through cooked honey, add ½ pound blanched toasted whole almonds, ¼ pound pine nuts and ¾ cup mixed diced candied fruit peel. Mold and garnish as for Struffoli.

UKRAINIAN CHRISTMAS EVE DOUGHNUTS

[*Pampushky*]

2 packages dry yeast
½ cup lukewarm water
1 tablespoon sugar
⅔ cup milk
¼ cup unsalted butter
1 teaspoon salt
⅓ cup sugar
2 whole eggs, beaten
3 egg yolks
1 teaspoon vanilla
Grated rind of 1 lemon
4 to 5 cups flour, as needed
Fillings: Prune jam (lekvar), or poppy seed filling, page 42, or cherry preserves, or apricot jam
Lard, for deep frying
Fine granulated sugar
Cinnamon

Sprinkle yeast into warm water, add 1 tablespoon sugar, cover lightly and set aside in a warm place for 5 or 10 minutes, or until mixture foams. Scald milk and stir in butter, salt and sugar. When butter melts, cool milk to lukewarm. Combine with beaten eggs and yolks and yeast mixture, vanilla and lemon rind. Gradually beat in enough flour to make a medium-firm dough that is still pliable. Knead until smooth and elastic—about 10 minutes. Place dough in a floured bowl, dust with flour and set to rise in a draft-free corner until double in bulk—about 1½ hours. Punch dough down and let it rise again until doubled.

Turn dough onto a floured board and roll out to ½-inch thickness. Cut into circles with a 3-inch round cookie cutter. Place a teaspoonful of filling on half of the circles. Top with unfilled circles and pinch edges closed, using a little cold water to seal them. Let rise, uncovered, on floured board until doubled in bulk. Fry a few at a time in lard heated to 375°. Turn once so both sides become golden brown. Allow about 6 minutes for frying each batch. Drain on paper towel and sprinkle with sugar and cinnamon.

Makes about 2 dozen doughnuts

DUTCH DOUGHNUTS

Oliebollen, the national pastry of Holland, are always served on December 6th, St. Nicholas' Eve. The dough is similar to that of the Pampushky but is a little puffier, as it is not rolled.

Follow preceding recipe, but use only 3 to 4 cups flour, 3 tablespoons sugar and 1 cup milk. When dough has risen for the second time, knead in ¼ cup raisins and ½ cup mixed diced candied fruit peels. Drop from a tablespoon into oil heated to 375° and fry. Sprinkle with cinnamon and sugar before serving.

Makes about 3 dozen doughnuts

PUDDINGS & DESSERTS

Chapter Five

"O, a wonderful pudding!"
No single dish is more synonymous with Christmas feasting than the English plum pudding, fragrant with spices, darkly rich with fruit and handsome with its sprig of holly and wreath of blue-burning brandy flames. This pudding, or "plum cake" as it used to be called, is older than even Bob Cratchit would have guessed when he sang its praise. It is, in fact, said to be older than Christmas itself, since at least a version of it was part of the Druid Yuletide celebration. Legend has it that Daga, the god of plenty, mixed a pudding of the best meats, fruits and spices the earth could offer, in celebration of the winter solstice.

The word "plum" used in the name of a pudding that usually contains none refers back to the time when its main ingredient was prunes, later replaced by raisins. English housewives used to prepare the pudding mixture on the last Sunday before Advent, known as "Stir-up Day" because the church Collect for that day began with "Stir up" and seemed to be a timely reminder of the task at hand. Each week another member of the family stirred up the pudding batch for luck, until it was steamed on Christmas morning. It is customary to hide small silver (never copper) coins and trinkets in the pudding as surprise gifts. Variations on the plum pudding theme are practically endless. Some steam for 7 or 8 hours. Others are aged weeks before they are cooked, and those adapted in our own country often include whiskey. The first recipe that follows is somewhat simplified but authentic. Baking powder and soda are not essential or traditional, but they do assure a lighter pudding. Although the pudding bag is the time-honored device for steaming, the basin or mold is easier to handle and results in a better shape.

CHRISTMAS PLUM PUDDING

[*England*]

- ⅔ cup chopped pitted prunes or dates
- ⅔ cup seedless dark raisins
- ⅔ cup golden raisins
- 3 tablespoons chopped crystallized ginger
- ⅔ cup currants
- ¼ cup each diced candied citron, orange peel and lemon peel
- ½ cup rum, brandy, Madeira or sherry
- 1½ cups stout, ale or beer
- ¼ pound beef suet, chopped
- 1½ cups dark brown sugar, firmly packed
- 4 eggs
- ½ cup ground blanched almonds
- 2 tart apples, peeled, cored and chopped
- 1 cup bread crumbs
- ¾ cup sifted flour
- 1 teaspoon salt
- 1½ teaspoons baking powder and ½ teaspoon baking soda
- 1 teaspoon cinnamon
- ⅛ teaspoon each cloves, allspice, nutmeg
- Grated rind of 1 orange
- Grated rind of 1 lemon
- 1 cup brandy, for flaming
- Sprig of holly
- Hard Sauce, page 210

Combine all dried and candied fruits, cover with brandy, rum, Madeira or sherry and stout, ale or beer and let stand 2 hours. Cream suet with sugar and beat in eggs. Mix with fruits and their soaking liquid. Add almonds, apple and bread crumbs. Resift flour with salt, baking powder and soda and spices. Add to first mixture with grated rind and stir well until completely mixed.

Turn mixture into one well-buttered 2-quart pudding mold or two 1-quart molds. Cover with aluminum foil or pudding cloth that has been wrung out in hot water. Tie cloth or foil securely. Place on rack in a kettle. Add enough boiling water to come two thirds of the way up sides of mold. Cover kettle and steam pudding for about 3 hours, or until firm. Add boiling water if needed to maintain level. Remove cover for 5 minutes before unmolding pudding. If left covered in the mold, this pudding can be stored for months in the refrigerator. Reheat by steaming for 1 hour.

To serve, invert hot pudding onto serving dish. Heat 1 cup

brandy, ignite and pour while burning over pudding. (The room is usually darkened to heighten this effect.) A sprig of holly stuck into the top of the pudding is the standard decoration and a hard sauce is the equally traditional accompaniment.

Makes 8 to 10 servings

JAMAICAN CHRISTMAS PUDDING

Follow preceding recipe, with these changes: Substitute ¾ cup chopped candied cherries for the prunes or dates; pecans for the almonds; pound cake or ladyfinger crumbs for the bread crumbs. Use rum to moisten fruits but eliminate beer. Add 1 cup of milk to the mixture just before dry ingredients are stirred in. Substitute butter for suet, creaming it with 1 cup granulated sugar; mix in ¼ cup dark molasses with eggs. Eliminate brown sugar. Steam, set aflame with dark rum and serve with hard sauce.

VICTORIAN CHRISTMAS PUDDING

[*England*]

For purists with patience . . .

- 1 pound beef suet, shredded
- 2 cups sifted flour
- 4½ cups bread crumbs
- 1 pound seedless black raisins
- 1 pound currants
- 1 pound sugar
- 2 cups mixed diced candied citron, orange and lemon peel
- 1 teaspoon grated nutmeg
- 2 teaspoons cinnamon
- 1 teaspoon mace
- ¼ cup blanched and slivered almonds
- ½ teaspoon salt
- Juice and grated rind of 1 lemon
- ⅓ cup brandy
- 8 eggs, well beaten
- Milk, only as needed
- Brandy, for flaming
- Hard Sauce, page 210

Dredge suet with a little flour. Combine with bread crumbs, remaining flour, raisins, currants, sugar, candied fruit peels, nutmeg, cinnamon, mace, almonds and salt. Toss together well until thoroughly mixed. Mix lemon juice and rind with brandy and eggs.

Stir into dry ingredients and set aside in a cool place for 4 or 5 hours. Stir in just enough milk (about ¼ cup) to make a stiff paste. Do not make pudding too wet or it will be heavy.

Turn into a well-buttered gallon-size pudding mold, or several smaller ones, dividing it any way you wish. Cover and place on rack in kettle. Add boiling water to come two thirds of the way up the side of the mold. Cover kettle and steam pudding for about 8 hours, or until firm. (Smaller puddings will take about 3 to 4 hours to steam, depending on size.) Add boiling water if necessary to maintain the level. Uncover to let steam escape before unmolding. If you want to store the pudding, uncover to let steam escape, recover and store in refrigerator. (It will keep for months. Steam for about 2 hours before serving.) Set aflame with warmed brandy and serve with sauce.

Makes about 24 servings

DEVONSHIRE BRANDY PUDDING

[*England*]

Cut leftover or canned plum pudding into long strips about ½ inch wide. Sprinkle with brandy or rum and stack them in an open lattice pattern in a pie plate or soufflé dish. Prepare your favorite baked cup custard mixture (the amount will depend on how much pudding you have left over) and flavor it with lemon rind and nutmeg. Pour over pudding strips, sprinkle with more nutmeg, set in a pan of water and bake as you would custard. Serve warm or chilled. Pudding may be unmolded or served from baking dish. For 1 pound of pudding, use a 6-cup soufflé dish and a custard mixture of 2 cups milk and 3 eggs.

COLONIAL VIRGINIA FROZEN PLUM PUDDING

- 1/4 cup chopped candied orange peel
- 1/4 cup chopped citron
- 1/4 cup chopped angelica
- 1/4 cup chopped candied cherries
- 1/4 cup raisins
- 1/4 cup sherry or Madeira
- 1/4 cup brandy or rum
- 3 cups milk
- 10 egg yolks
- 2 cups sugar
- Pinch of salt
- 3 cups heavy sweet cream, whipped
- 2/3 cup crushed bitter Italian macaroons (Amaretti)
- 1/3 cup blanched chopped almonds
- Whipped cream and whole candied cherries

Combine all fruits and soak for 1 hour in mixture of sherry or Madeira and rum or brandy. Beat milk with egg yolks, sugar and salt and cook over low heat, stirring constantly, until mixture is thick enough to coat the back of a metal spoon. Cool. Turn whipped cream into cooled custard, sprinkle with macaroons and almonds, add fruits with liquid in which they soaked, and fold all together gently but thoroughly. Pour into a chilled and rinsed 3-quart bombe mold that has a tight-fitting lid. A mold that is tiered and fluted is perfect for this—the fancier the better. Cover and place in freezer for about 7 hours, or until frozen.

To unmold, uncover and wipe bombe mold with a cloth wrung out in very hot water. Loosen edges with a sharp knife and invert onto serving platter. Decorate with whipped cream and candied cherries and/or sprigs of holly.

Makes about 15 servings

Note: Naturally, you can make half of this amount and use a 1½-quart mold, but it is not nearly as impressive-looking.

BOULE DE NEIGE

[*France*]

The classic French ice cream "snowball" has in recent years become a favorite dessert at elegant Christmas dinners. The preceding recipe is perfect for making this. Prepare the mixture and turn into a chilled and rinsed 3-quart spherical bombe mold. Chill. Unmold onto a chilled platter. Put 3 cups of slightly sweetened whipped cream in a pastry bag, and using a fancy tube, force out small whipped-cream rosettes all over the frozen-cream sphere. It should be completely covered, so place rosettes close together. Decorate with sprigs of holly. Again, half of this amount can be made in a 1½-quart mold.

The following two recipes are from The Shaker Cookbook, *by Caroline B. Piercy.*

SHAKER BREAD AND BUTTER PUDDING

"Butter an ample baking dish. Cover the bottom with fairly thick slices of bread generously buttered. Then add a goodly layer of currants, also one of shredded citron, of candied orange peel and candied lemon peel. Then spread with a layer of strawberry jam, not too thin, for remember it is Christmas! Then repeat these layers until the dish is two thirds filled. Then pour over this an unboiled custard made of plenty of eggs and rich milk; remember it is Christmas! Let stand for at least two hours. Then add a pretty fluting of your best pastry around the very edge of the dish; this touch is not necessary but it adds much to the gaiety of the dish. Bake until crust is well set and top is a rich and appetizing golden brown. Eat it with much relish, for remember it is Christmas!"

SHAKER CHRISTMAS PUDDING

- 2 pounds raisins
- ½ pint red wine or apple cider
- 1 pound chopped suet
- 12 eggs, separated
- 2 cups milk
- ½ cup maple syrup
- 8 cups flour
- 1½ teaspoons salt
- 1 teaspoon mace
- 1 tablespoon cinnamon
- 1 tablespoon ginger
- Hard Sauce, page 210, or Shaker Excellent Pudding Sauce, page 211

Soak raisins overnight in wine or boiled cider. Drain well, reserving both fruit and soaking liquid. Cream suet. Beat egg yolks into milk along with maple syrup. Combine this mixture with flour, salt, spices, raisins and wine or cider and suet. Beat egg whites until stiff. Fold into mixture, gently but thoroughly, using a rubber spatula. Turn mixture into a pudding bag that has been wet, wrung out and lightly floured, or into a well-buttered 3-quart pudding mold. If you are using a bag or open pudding basin, do not tie cloth too tightly, as pudding will swell. If you are using a mold, be sure pudding does not fill it more than two thirds of the way.

Place tied bag in boiling water, cover kettle and boil for 3 hours. If you are using a mold, cover tightly and stand it on a rack in a kettle and add enough boiling water to reach two thirds of the way up mold. Cover kettle and steam for 3 to 4 hours. Open cover and let steam escape for 5 minutes before unmolding. Serve with either sauce.

AMBROSIA

A traditional dessert for Christmas dinner in the southern part of the United States, most especially in Georgia and South Carolina. Although not strictly authentic, a little orange liqueur or kirsch, sprinkled over each layer of pineapple or oranges, adds a very flavorful and mellowing touch.

6 to 8 eating oranges, preferably navels
1 large ripe pineapple, peeled and shredded or diced
½ to 1 cup very fine granulated sugar
4 cups shredded coconut, preferably fresh
½ cup each Kirsch and Grand Marnier

Remove peel and white underskin from oranges and cut crosswise into thin round slices. Arrange alternate layers of orange slices, pineapple and coconut in a glass bowl, sprinkling about a tablespoonful of sugar and some of the liqueurs over each layer of oranges. End with top layer of coconut. Chill 4 to 5 hours before serving.

Serves 8 to 10

APPLE AND ORANGE FLORENTINE

[*England*]

This favorite combination of spiced ale and apples appears again in this deep-dish tart, a Christmas specialty of Bedfordshire. It originated in Tuscany, where Chianti undoubtedly preceded ale.

6 large baking apples, such as Northern Spies or Rome Beauties
7 tablespoons unsalted butter
6 tablespoons brown sugar
2 teaspoons cinnamon
Grated rind of 1 lemon
4 tablespoons orange marmalade
½ recipe for Epiphany tart pastry, page 81
1 egg yolk beaten with 1 tablespoon water
2 cups ale
1 stick cinnamon
4 or 5 cloves
½ teaspoon each nutmeg and allspice
Heavy sweet cream

Wash apples and dry them thoroughly. Do not peel. Remove cores, being careful not to cut through bottom of apple. Cream butter with sugar, cinnamon and lemon rind. Place a little butter mixture in the hollow of each apple, add marmalade and top with a bit more butter. Dot extra butter on top of apples. Stand apples close together in a buttered soufflé dish just large enough to hold the apples upright but without packing them too close together. Roll out a round of pastry dough to fit the top of the baking dish. Place over apples but do not seal edges to pan. Brush with egg yolk. Bake in preheated 425° oven for 10 minutes, reduce heat to 350° and continue baking for about 20 minutes, or until crust is crisp and golden brown.

Meanwhile, heat, but do not boil, ale with cinnamon, cloves, nutmeg and allspice. Steep for 10 minutes. Remove cinnamon and cloves. When tart is done, carefully lift off crust without breaking it. Pour ale into baking dish, cut crust in 6 wedge-shaped portions and replace a wedge over each apple. Or place each wedge in a deep dessert plate and top with an apple and combined ale and pan juices. Serve very hot with cold sweet cream on the side.

Makes 6 servings

CHRISTMAS EVE NOODLES WITH POPPY SEEDS

[*Poland—Kluski z Makiem; Hungary—Mákos Csusza*]

1 pound wide egg noodles
1 cup milk or water
1 cup blanched, dried and ground poppy seeds
½ cup sugar or 2 tablespoons honey, or combination of both

Cook noodles until tender in boiling salted water to cover. Drain. Scald milk or water and mix into poppy seeds with sugar and/or honey to taste. Simmer for 5 minutes, stir into noodles and serve hot.

Makes about 8 servings

CHRISTMAS EVE BISCUITS WITH POPPY SEEDS

[*Hungary—Makosgubo*]

1 envelope dry yeast
2 tablespoons lukewarm water
1 teaspoon sugar
¾ cup milk
½ teaspoon salt
¼ cup unsalted butter
¼ cup sugar
2 whole eggs, beaten
3 egg yolks, beaten
2 to 2½ cups flour, as needed
⅓ cup unsalted butter
½ cup sugar, approximately
½ cup washed, dried and ground poppy seeds

Sprinkle yeast into lukewarm water, add 1 teaspoon sugar and set aside in a warm place for 5 to 10 minutes, or until mixture is foamy. Scald milk, add salt, butter, ¼ cup sugar and stir until butter melts. Cool to lukewarm. Add to yeast mixture along with beaten whole eggs and yolks. Stir in 1 cup flour. Mix thoroughly, cover loosely and set to rise in a draft-free corner for about 30 minutes, or until dough is light and puffy.

Beat in as much remaining flour as needed to make dough smooth but soft. Knead for 10 minutes, or until smooth and elastic. Place in floured bowl, dust top of dough with flour, cover loosely and set to rise in a draft-free corner until double in bulk—about 1 to 1½ hours.

Punch dough down, knead for 2 or 3 minutes, then cut off pieces slightly smaller than walnuts. Roll into balls, dredge lightly with flour, dusting off excess, and place 1 inch apart on a buttered baking sheet. Let rise for 30 minutes. Bake in preheated 300° oven for 1 hour, or until pale golden brown around edges. Place biscuits in a bowl, blanch with boiling water and drain immediately. Heat ⅓ cup butter in a large skillet over low heat, add biscuits and stir gently with a wooden spoon to coat with butter. Sprinkle with sugar and ground poppy seeds and serve while hot.

Makes about 4 dozen biscuits

LITHUANIAN PRESKUCIAI SLIZIKAI

Follow preceding recipe, using 2 whole eggs and no yolks and only 2 tablespoons butter. After dough has risen for the second time, roll it out to ½-inch thickness, cut into ½-inch-wide strips and cut these into pieces a little less than ½ inch long. Bake as described, and serve these biscuits with the sauce below.

Poppy Seed Milk: Soak ½ pound poppy seeds in boiling water until they can be crushed between your fingers. Dry and pound or grind. Add 12 blanched and finely chopped almonds, grated rind of 1 lemon, sugar and/or honey to taste. Chill and mix with 2 cups light sweet cream or milk.

POLISH TRIANGLE COOKIES WITH POPPY SEEDS

[*Lamance*]

2⅔ cups flour
¼ cup unsalted butter
½ cup plus 1 tablespoon confectioners' sugar
1 egg yolk
1 tablespoon vodka or gin
Grated rind of ½ lemon
½ teaspoon salt
½ cup sour cream, or as needed
Poppy Seed Milk, above, made with only ½ cup heavy cream

Place flour in a wide bowl and cut in butter, using two knives or a pastry blender, until mixture resembles coarse meal. Add sugar, egg yolk, vodka or gin, lemon rind and salt and toss together. Gradually add and stir in just enough sour cream to make a dough that can be kneaded. Knead on floured board, pounding vigorously to make dough smooth and firm. Roll out to paper thinness, cut into triangles 1 to 1½ inches long and place on lightly buttered baking sheet. Bake in preheated 350° oven for about 10 minutes, or until crisp and pale gold. Remove from pan and cool.

Prepare the poppy-seed mixture. This will be much thicker than in the Lithuanian version. Turn into a serving dish and garnish with a border of the cookies. Serve additional cookies on the side.

Makes 6 to 8 servings

COCONUT RICE PUDDING

This sweet rice, Arroz con Dulce, is a year-round dessert in South America. In Puerto Rico it is a must on every Christmas and Epiphany table.

5 to 6 cups coconut milk, page 242
1 cup rice
1 teaspoon salt
¼ teaspoon powdered ginger, or ½-inch piece fresh ginger root
¼ teaspoon crushed anise seeds (optional)
½ teaspoon cinnamon
½ teaspoon powdered cloves
½ cup raisins
1 cup sugar
Cinnamon and cassava or manioc flour (optional), for sprinkling

Place 4 cups coconut milk in the top of a double boiler and bring to a boil. Rinse rice in boiling water and drain well. Add rice to boiling coconut milk with salt and spices. Cover and cook slowly for about 1 hour, stirring occasionally until rice is tender and mixture is thick. Add hot coconut milk if pudding looks dry. Add raisins, 1 cup coconut milk and sugar. Stir and cook slowly for another 15 to 20 minutes, or until pudding is very soft and creamy. Pour into a serving dish, chill and sprinkle with cinnamon and, if you like, cassava before serving.

Serves 6–8

Variation: In Panama and many other parts of Latin America, this pudding is made without any spices cooked into it. Only cinnamon is sprinkled on top before serving. Raisins may be omitted. If you do not want to bother with coconut milk, there is an easier way if you can get canned Cream of Coconut, usually available in any Spanish neighborhood. It is a sweet, syrupy coconut extract. Substitute whole milk for coconut milk. When rice is tender, add 1 extra cup milk, raisins and, instead of sugar, ¾ cup Cream of Coconut, or to taste. Continue cooking as described.

GOLDEN EGG THREADS

[*Brazil and Portugal—Fios de Ovos*]

This is an unusual and beautiful dessert that requires a great deal of skill to make. It is usually left to professional *pâtissiers,* but if you are adventuresome, you might like to try your hand at it. Oddly enough, the identical dessert is served in Thailand, though, of course, it has nothing to do with Christmas. I have not been able to track down any relationship, but perhaps the link was the early Portuguese traders or missionaries.

16 very fresh egg yolks
2 whole eggs
8 cups sugar
2 cups water
1 teaspoon rose water or orange-flower water
Ice water

Combine yolks and whole eggs, stirring with a wooden spoon. Do not beat. Strain to remove white threads and "eyes." While you are preparing eggs, cook sugar and water with rose water or orange-flower water until mixture threads, or reaches 220° on a candy thermometer.

Remove 1 cup of syrup and add it to a bowl of ice water. Keep remaining syrup boiling. Using a small funnel (in Brazil and Portugal, a special three-spouted funnel is used), fill it with egg mixture, holding your finger over the opening of the spout. Open the spout just enough for a very thin stream of egg to thread its way down into the boiling syrup. If you cannot get the stream of egg thin enough, pierce an empty egg shell with a needle and trickle egg mixture through that. Using a slotted spoon, remove cooked threads as they float to the surface (about 2 to 3 minutes) and place them in ice water and syrup combination for 5 minutes. Drain in a colander. Repeat until all egg mixture is cooked. Add water if syrup thickens too much during cooking and keep it at a constant temperature. Mold threads into custard cups or in one 6-cup soufflé dish. Chill overnight and unmold by inverting onto dessert or serving plates. Or use to decorate cakes and puddings.

Makes 6 to 8 servings

DANISH RICE PORRIDGE

[Julerisengrod]

A Christmas Eve treat throughout Scandinavia, this porridge contains one almond as a token of good fortune for the person who finds it. This Danish version is the richest. In that country some of this porridge is left in front of each door or in the attic to feed the Julenissen, the Christmas elves who watch over animals, most especially cats.

2 cups raw long-grained rice
2½ quarts milk
1 whole blanched almond
½ cup heavy sweet cream
½ teaspoon salt
Butter, cinnamon and sugar
3 cups nonalcoholic malt beer or raspberry syrup (optional)
1 cup water

Scald rice with boiling water. Drain and repeat with fresh boiling water. Heat milk in the top of a double boiler. When simmering, stir in rice gradually, so that milk does not stop cooking. Stir with a wooden spoon until milk boils. Reduce heat, cover and cook rice slowly until very soft—about 1 to 1½ hours—stirring occasionally to prevent sticking. Remove from heat and stir in almond, cream and salt. Serve in warm cereal or cream-soup bowls. Garnish each portion with a generous knob of butter and a sprinkling of cinnamon and sugar. Heat malt beer or raspberry syrup with water. Pour over porridge.

Makes 6 to 8 servings

GOLDEN WHEAT AND APRICOT PILAF

[Armenia—Anoush Abour]

This recipe for "Sweet Soup" came from Sayat Nova, a restaurant where Arshag Tarpinian and his mother used to turn out the best Armenian food in New York. Although currants and prunes are sometimes added to this dessert, Mrs. Tarpinian prefers it without those fruits, as she says they darken the wheat. What's good enough for her is good enough for me. Similar sweet wheat porridges are served in several other countries, as you can see from the variations that follow. All of these are based on the whole wheat kernels which are available at health food shops and at Armenian grocery stores, where they are called *gorgod.* The grain may be soaked overnight to cut cooking time, if you find that more convenient.

3 cups whole grain wheat
1 teaspoon salt, or as needed
1 cup golden raisins
½ cup pine nuts
½ cup chopped, blanched walnuts
½ cup blanched halved almonds
10 to 12 dried apricots, each cut in quarters
1 cup sugar or ½ cup sugar and ½ cup honey, or to taste
3 or 4 drops rose water (optional)
Cinnamon
Sugar
Chopped walnuts, almonds or pistachio nuts

Wash grain thoroughly in boiling water. Drain well and place in a heavy saucepan with 8 cups of boiling water. Cover tightly and simmer slowly until grain is completely tender—this will take about 4 to 6 hours, depending on the quality of the grain. Add more boiling water if necessary. Toward the end of the cooking time, stir in just enough salt to eliminate the watery flavor. This should cook to a porridge consistency, with all of the water absorbed by the time the grain is done. If there is excess water, drain it off. With grain over low heat, stir in raisins, pine nuts, walnuts, almonds, apricots and sugar, or sugar and honey, and rose water. Stir until all sugar is dissolved and mixture is thick and moist. Remove from heat, turn into individual custard cups or dessert dishes, or into one large serving bowl, and chill thoroughly. Stir and serve sprinkled with cinnamon, sugar and chopped nuts.

Makes 8 to 10 servings, unless you are feeding Armenians, in which case this will be enough for 4 to 6

KAMHIÉ

[*Lebanon and Syria*]

In the Levant, the Christmas holiday begins on December 4th with the feast of St. Barbara, who shared her bread with the poor, and Kamhié is the dish that is served that night. Follow the preceding recipe, but with these changes: candied fruit peel or crushed sugar candy is added and dried apricots are not generally used. All other ingredients are included and a little orange-flower water may be added along with the rose water. As the wheat cooks, the head of the house is supposed to recite the story of St. Barbara to his guests.

KUTYA

[*Russia, Ukraine and Poland*]

In the Ukraine some of the Kutya is placed outdoors for Father Frost, as a bribe to keep him from freezing the crops. Another portion is tossed up to the ceiling, and the number of grains that stick indicates how many bees the farmer will have in his hive next year. Finally, when everyone has eaten his fill, a spoon is left in the remaining Kutya so departed spirits may feed themselves if they return on Christmas Eve.

Cook wheat as described in basic recipe on opposite page. Mix with 2 to 3 cups honey and simmer 5 to 10 minutes. Stir in 1½ cups blanched, dried and ground poppy seeds and chill. Sprinkle with chopped almonds or walnuts before serving. You may also add ¼ cup sweet cream to the poppy seeds before they are stirred into the wheat.

MOTE CON HUESILLOS

[*Chile*]

This is a Chilean Christmas dessert that is surprisingly similar to the Golden Wheat and Apricot Pilaf on page 155. It is made with cooked hominy (coarse white cornmeal) which is chilled and served with stewed dried apricots (huesillos). The apricot nectar is served in a glass with the cut fruit in it.

HONDURAN TORRIJAS

Although this dessert is a standard in Spain, Mexico and Latin America for many festive occasions, it is a special favorite in Honduras at Christmas. It is very much like Puerto Rican and Cuban Sopa Borracha, "drunken soup," or the Portuguese Rabanadas, pieces of wine- or whiskey-soaked pound cake dipped in egg and fried.

1 pound sponge cake or lady-fingers
6 eggs, separated
Lard or oil, for deep frying
9 cups sugar
3 cups boiling water
1 2-inch piece cinnamon stick
1/3 cup port or Malaga wine
Powdered cinnamon
Chopped almonds or pine nuts (optional)

Cut cake into slices about 1/3 inch thick, or split ladyfingers. Beat egg yolks until foamy. Beat whites until stiff and fold into yolks. Spread egg mixture on both sides of cake slices or ladyfinger halves. Heat lard or oil to 375° and fry cake, turning once so both sides become golden brown—this will take 3 or 4 minutes. Drain on paper toweling. Place cake in serving dish that has a rim. Boil sugar and water until a syrup is formed—about 10 minutes. Add cinnamon stick and wine and simmer 3 or 4 minutes longer. Remove cinnamon and pour syrup over cake. Sprinkle with cinnamon and nuts. Let stand 5 minutes and serve hot.

Makes 8 to 10 servings

Variation: If you prefer, the cake can be soaked in wine before it is spread with butter and fried. In that case omit wine from syrup.

PRUNE AND WALNUT DUMPLINGS

[*Poland—Pierozki; Ukraine—Vareniki; Czechoslovakia—Knedli; Hungary—Szilvasgomboc*]

FILLING:

1 to 1½ pounds prunes
Sugar cubes
Cinnamon

DOUGH:

1 egg
½ cup water
1 teaspoon salt
2 cups flour, or as needed

TOPPING:

⅓ cup chopped walnuts
⅓ cup sugar
Cinnamon (optional)

Soak prunes in hot water for 1 hour. Remove pits but leave prunes whole. Press ½ cube sugar and a little cinnamon into the cavity of each prune.

Combine egg, water and salt and add enough flour to make a soft but not sticky dough. Knead for 3 to 5 minutes on a floured board until dough is smooth but not stiff. Divide dough in half, cover with waxed paper and let it rest for 15 minutes. Roll out each half as thin as possible and cut in circles that will fit around the prunes. Wrap a circle (or square) of dough around each prune and pinch edges closed.

Drop a few dumplings at a time into a large potful of rapidly boiling salted water. Keep uncooked dumplings covered with a towel to prevent drying. As dumplings puff up and cook (about 4 minutes), remove with a slotted spoon and drain in a colander. Continue cooking until all are done. Serve hot, sprinkled with chopped nuts, sugar and cinnamon.

Makes about 20 dumplings

Variation: In the Ukraine and Czechoslovakia, bread crumbs browned in butter and sour cream are the traditional accompaniments to these dumplings. If you like, some chopped walnuts can be used to fill prunes along with the cinnamon and sugar.

POPPY SEED DUMPLINGS

Follow preceding recipe for dough. Prepare filling described for Poppy Seed Horseshoe, page 42. Place a heaping teaspoonful on each circle or square of dough; close and cook.

PRUNE JAM DUMPLINGS

Follow recipe for dough, page 159. Fill each circle or square with 1 rounded teaspoonful thick prune jam (lekvar) to which you can add a little lemon juice, cinnamon and chopped walnuts, to taste; close and cook. Sugar is rarely needed, as the jam is already sweetened.

CHRISTMAS DISH

This was a specialty of Victorian England. Crumble macaroons and ladyfingers into bottom of bowl. Combine 1 cup red currant jelly, 1 cup sherry, 1 cup raisin wine and 2 tablespoons fine granulated sugar and bring to a boil in a heavy-bottomed saucepan. Stir until jelly melts and sugar is dissolved. Pour boiling over cake crumbs and let stand in a cool place for 1½ hours. Cover with custard, as in next recipe, or with thick layer of whipped cream. Decorate with blanched whole almonds.

WASSAIL CUSTARD

[*England*]

Basically a trifle, this was a Christmas favorite in Victorian times.

BASE:

12 macaroons
12 ladyfingers, or comparable strips of sponge cake
¼ cup sherry, Madeira or raisin wine
¼ cup brandy
Juice of 1 lemon

CUSTARD:

6 egg yolks
¾ cup sugar
Pinch of salt
½ cup sherry or Madeira
1 tablespoon plus 1 teaspoon flour
5 egg whites, stiffly beaten

TOPPING:

Blanched whole almonds, toasted or untoasted
Nutmeg
Confectioners' sugar
Whipped cream (optional)

Cover the bottom of a big glass serving dish or bowl with a mixture of crumbled macaroons and ladyfingers. Moisten thoroughly with wine, brandy and lemon juice. Set aside in a cool place for 1 hour. Meanwhile, beat egg yolks with sugar, salt and wine. Cook in the top of a double boiler over 1 inch of simmering water until mixture is thick and frothy. Stir in flour and cook, stirring, for 2 to 3 minutes. Cool custard and fold whites in gently but thoroughly. Pour over crumbled cake and decorate with almonds and a sprinkling of nutmeg and sugar. Let stand in a cool place for 1 hour. If you like, whipped cream can be spread or piped on top of custard and can then be decorated with the almonds, nutmeg and sugar.

Makes 6 to 8 servings

CANDIES & CONFECTIONS

Chapter Six

Almond Paste and Marzipan

Although these terms are generally used interchangeably, almond paste consists of ground blanched almonds and sugar. To make marzipan, add lightly beaten egg whites, extra sugar and a flavoring such as rose water, orange-flower water or lemon juice, as in the recipe below. It is marzipan that is shaped into candies or baked into cookies, and, generally, it is the almond paste that is used as filling for cakes and breads. The Crusaders brought this confection to Italy from the Middle East, in the form of coins called "marchpane," a word derived from the Arabic. Few countries would consider Christmas complete without it. It is usually molded into fruit or vegetables, or, in Denmark, into little pink pigs. Germans are fond of forming small cookies with it and then baking them, and in Spain and South America, it is considered a form of Torrone (page 172). The most famous marzipan-producing cities of the world are Lübeck and Königsberg in Germany and Odense in Denmark.

One of the nicest Christmas customs I know is the Danish marzipan party, which can take place any time during the two weeks before December 25th. Guests are invited for the evening and each is given a supply of prepared marzipan along with all sorts of decorative bits and pieces—chocolate and colored sugar sprinkles, silver shot, raisins and currants, red cinnamon drops, nut meats, cocoa, cinnamon, shredded coconut, etc. Each person then shapes the paste into forms and decorates them accordingly. A prize goes to the best sculpture of the evening, and as all are provided with plenty of aquavit, the proceedings become rather gay. Guests take their works of art home and hang them on the tree or place them under it.

Both almond paste and marzipan can be purchased in cans or rolls. Be sure you know which you have before using in a recipe.

ALMOND PASTE

2 cups blanched almonds
2 cups sugar

Grind almonds 4 or 5 times through the finest blade of the food chopper or in a nut grinder to a smooth and slightly oily consistency. Work in sugar (the mixture will be like thick, wet sand). The almonds may be ground in a blender or food processor; grind ½ cup at a time together with 1 tablespoon of the sugar, working in remaining sugar when all the nuts have been ground. Store in an airtight container. Use mixture to fill pastry or candies or to make marzipan (below).

Makes about 1 pound

MARZIPAN

1 cup Almond Paste (above)
1 egg white
1 cup sifted confectioners' sugar
Few drops of rose water or orange-flower water or lemon juice

Mash paste until slightly softened. Beat egg white until fluffy and blend in. Add sugar and flavoring and mix in until smooth enough to handle, adding more sugar if mixture is too sticky, or lemon juice if it crumbles. Knead for a minute or two until smooth and then shape as desired.

Marzipan Fruit and Vegetables: Color marzipan with appropriate food coloring. Shape by hand or in small tart or marzipan molds. Dry on racks and store in airtight containers.

Marzipan Potatoes: Roll marzipan into balls ¾ to 1 inch in diameter. With a toothpick prick small holes or "eyes" into the surface of the ball. Roll in unsweetened cocoa until well covered on all sides.

Danish Marzipan Pigs: Color marzipan pale pink and shape into pigs about 2 inches long. Use poppy seeds, silver shot or chocolate sprinkles for eyes. Dry and store as above.

Chocolate-Covered Marzipan: Dip shaped marzipan (fruits, pigs, balls, square or finger-shaped bars) into Easiest Chocolate Icing, page 204. Dry on rack and wrap each piece in plastic wrap.

Baked Marzipan: Divide marzipan into small portions and roll each in thin pencil strips. Turn into circles or pretzel shapes about 1 to 2 inches across and press to flatten slightly. Or roll or press marzipan to ¼-inch thickness between two sheets of waxed paper. Remove top paper and cut shapes with small fancy cookie cutters. Dry in warm room overnight. Brush with egg yolk and bake in preheated 450° oven for 10 to 15 minutes, or until golden brown on top.

Lübeck Marzipan Heart: You can make this in any size you like. Press marzipan paste into a heart-shaped cookie cutter set on a buttered baking sheet. Marzipan should be about ½ inch thick. Reserve a little of the paste and use to form a crimped edge and cut out leaves around the heart. Brush edges and raised decorations with beaten egg yolk. Bake in preheated 350° oven for 10 to 12 minutes, or until golden brown around edges. Remove cookie cutter and decorate with candied cherry halves and bits of angelica and other candied fruit peel by dipping these into egg white and placing them on the warm marzipan.

Makes enough for one 3½- to 4-inch heart

BALTHAZARS

[*Eastern Europe*]

This creamy chocolate confection is named for the dark-skinned Balthazar, the Ethiopian Wise Man who brought the gift of myrrh to the Christ Child. Caspar and Melchior, the other Magi, apparently have not inspired any Christmas recipes, or, at least, none I could find.

8 ounces (squares) semisweet chocolate
1 pound shelled walnuts
½ cup plus 1 tablespoon confectioners' sugar
1½ tablespoons rum
1 tablespoon grated orange rind
1 to 2 egg whites, as needed

Grate fine the chocolate and half of the walnuts. Remaining walnuts should be more coarsely chopped or grated. Mix chocolate and finely grated walnuts. Add sugar, rum and rind. Stir in enough egg white to make a smooth mixture that can be firmly packed. If mixture is too wet, add a little more sugar or nuts. Chill for 30 minutes; then divide in halves or thirds and form long rolls, each about 1 inch in diameter. Dredge rolls in the coarsely chopped walnuts, wrap in waxed paper and chill for at least 2 days. Cut in thin slices just before serving. Do not slice more candy than you need, as it can be stored for weeks if it is kept wrapped in waxed paper and chilled.

Makes about three 8-inch rolls or 6 to 8 dozen slices

CHOCOLATE TRUFFLES

[*France—Truffettes de Chambéry*]

Although moderately popular the year round, this confection appears as though by magic everywhere in Paris during the holiday season.

6 ounces (squares) dark semi-sweet chocolate
3 tablespoons unsalted butter
2 tablespoons confectioners' sugar
3 egg yolks
1 tablespoon rum or brandy
½ cup finely grated semisweet chocolate

Melt chocolate in the top of a double boiler, set over boiling water. Beat in butter and sugar and keep stirring until sugar dissolves. Remove from heat and add egg yolks, one at a time, beating well between additions. Stir in rum or brandy. Turn into a bowl, cover with waxed paper and set aside overnight in a cool dry place. Do not chill. Shape into balls about 1 inch in diameter. Roll in grated chocolate. Eat within a day or two.

Makes about 2 dozen truffles, depending on size

TARTUFI DI CIOCCOLATA

[*Italy*]

Follow preceding recipe, but roll balls in unsweetened cocoa. Black coffee is sometimes used as a flavoring instead of the rum or brandy.

CANDIED FRUIT PEEL

[*Europe*]

4 large grapefruit, or 6 navel oranges
3¼ cups sugar, approximately
2 teaspoons powdered ginger (optional)

Select ripe fruit with skins as near perfect as possible. Cut grapefruit or oranges in half and scrape out fruit pulp and membranes. (Or use reserved shells from grapefruit or oranges that have been eaten.) Be sure that all membranes are removed but leave white underskin on peel. Cut peel into long strips ¼ to ½ inch wide. Blanch in boiling water for 5 minutes. Drain and repeat blanching 3 times, using fresh boiling water each time.

Cook 2½ cups sugar in 1¼ cups boiling water until a light syrup forms. Add ginger and peels and stir through syrup. Simmer gently, partially covered, for about 40 minutes, or until peels have absorbed liquid and are tender. Place peels in a single layer on a sheet of waxed paper. Cool slightly and dredge with remaining sugar. Let dry in a warm room overnight. Store in airtight containers. Serve as candy or use in recipes. Cook orange and grapefruit peels separately to retain flavor of each.

Makes about 1½ pounds

HUNGARIAN CHESTNUT BONBONS

[*Gesztenyegolyok*]

One of the more elegant holiday treats given out at smart Budapest restaurants were marvelous rum-flavored chestnut-shaped bonbons made of puréed chestnuts encased in a glassy sugar coating. To make these requires the skill of a professional *pâtissier,* but with this recipe you can approximate these confections.

1½ pounds chestnuts, boiled, shelled and skinned
1 tablespoon rum or brandy
2¼ cups sugar
⅓ cup water
1 tablespoon light corn syrup
Vanilla Sugar (confectioners'), page 211

Purée chestnuts in a food mill, processor or through a sieve, and mix in rum to taste. Combine sugar, the water and corn syrup in a small heavy-bottomed saucepan and bring to a boil. Boil slowly, uncovered and without stirring, until mixture forms a hard ball when a little is dropped into cold water, or until it reaches 270° on a candy thermometer. Stir syrup into chestnuts, and when mixture is cool enough to touch, roll it into chestnut shapes. Dredge with sugar, cool completely, dredge with a little more sugar and wrap each chestnut in bright foil.

Makes about 6 dozen bonbons

DUTCH FUDGE

[*Roomborstplaat*]

Although fudge is popular in many countries during the Christmas season, it seems to have a special significance in Holland on December 6th, St. Nicholas' Eve. (It is a harder, less creamy fudge than we are familiar with.)

(continued)

¾ cup half-and-half (milk and cream)
1 cup plus 2 tablespoons granulated sugar
1 cup light brown sugar, firmly packed
1 tablespoon unsalted butter
Pinch of salt
1 tablespoon instant cocoa or instant coffee powder

This candy can be made either in small fancy shapes or cut into squares or diamonds. To make the fancy shapes, use about fifteen 1½-inch cookie cutters. Spread inside of each cutter with butter and place, cutting edge down, on a sheet of well-buttered waxed paper. If you do not use cookie cutters, butter the inside of a 9-inch flan ring and set it on buttered waxed paper; or butter the bottom and sides of a 9-inch round or square cake pan. Line bottom with buttered piece of waxed paper cut to fit exactly. Paper should not extend up the sides of the pan.

Scald half-and-half in a large heavy-bottomed saucepan. Remove from heat, add remaining ingredients and stir until sugar dissolves and butter melts. Bring to a boil over moderately high heat, stirring constantly. Wash sides of pan with a wet pastry brush. Cover and simmer for 3 to 5 minutes, or until all sugar crystals melt down from sides of pan. Uncover and continue cooking over moderate heat without stirring until mixture forms a soft ball when a little of it is dropped in ice water, or until it reaches 238° on a candy thermometer. Beat with a wooden spoon until mixture cools and thickens.

Pour candy, ⅓ inch thick, into forms. Let dry until hard—about 1 hour. Lift cookie cutters or flan ring off candy. Or turn candy out of lined layer-cake pan and remove paper. Cut into squares or diamond shapes, unless you have used the cookie cutters. Pack in airtight boxes lined with waxed paper. Place a sheet of waxed paper between layers.

Makes about 1 pound

Variations: This fudge can be made in other flavors. Follow the recipe, omitting coffee or chocolate. When cooked mixture has cooled slightly, stir in 2 teaspoons extract of vanilla, almond, lemon, orange or other fruit flavors.

To make a slightly creamier fudge, add ¼ teaspoon cream of tartar.

A nut meat can be pressed into the center of each piece of candy before it has hardened. This is especially good with chocolate, coffee and almond flavors.

MOLASSES TAFFY

The European version of this candy is generally made with white sugar, whereas in the United States, and especially in the South, it is almost always made with brown.

2 cups very dark molasses
1 cup brown sugar, firmly packed, or granulated sugar
1 tablespoon vinegar
2 tablespoons unsalted butter

Combine molasses, sugar and vinegar in a small heavy-bottomed saucepan and stir over low heat until sugar dissolves. Cover pan and boil without stirring until mixture reaches 245° on a candy thermometer or forms a firm ball when a little is dropped into cold water. Stir in butter and simmer slowly until mixture crackles when a little is dropped into cold water, or reaches 270° on a candy thermometer. Pour into a buttered pan or onto a marble slab.

When taffy is cool enough to handle, spread a little bland oil on your hands, and taking a small amount of taffy at a time, stretch it to about a 14-inch length; fold it back on itself and pull again. Continue until all of the taffy has been pulled to a point where it is creamy, light in color and no longer transparent and the ends hold a shape. Stretch to a ½-inch diameter, and using a pair of oiled scissors, cut into small squares or twist and form sticks or circles. Cool on a rack until hardened and wrap in waxed paper.

Makes about 1 pound

TORRONE

[*Italy*]

The sweet, chewy white candy that is Torrone to the Italians, Turron to the Iberians and South Americans, and Nougat to the French, is ubiquitous during the Christmas holidays in all of those areas. This original and most popular version, Torrone di Cremona, is said to have been invented by monks in the bell tower (torre) of the Cremona Cathedral.

Do not attempt to make this on a damp day.

Bakers' rice wafers, page 242, or confectioners' sugar
1 cup pure honey
3 egg whites
1 cup sugar
¾ cup toasted blanched almonds
1 cup toasted hazelnuts, with skins rubbed off
½ cup diced candied orange peel
Grated rind of 1 lemon
1 teaspoon vanilla, almond or lemon extract, or 2 tablespoons rum, brandy or orange liqueur

The honey, to thicken properly, must be pure, not adulterated with chemicals. To be sure that you have such honey, buy one that is imported, or better yet, get it in a health-food store.

If you can get the wafers, butter two 8-inch square cake pans and line with them. If not, butter pans, line with a double thickness of waxed paper and sprinkle liberally with confectioners' sugar.

Cook honey in the top of a double boiler, over boiling water, until it forms a soft ball when a little is dropped into cold water, or until it reaches 237° to 239° on a candy thermometer. Beat egg whites until stiff and gradually pour in caramelized honey, beating constantly.

Meanwhile, cook sugar with 2 tablespoons water in a heavy-bottomed saucepan until mixture caramelizes. Pour slowly into egg-honey mixture, beating constantly. You must work quickly all during this so that mixture does not cool and harden. Turn back into top of double boiler and cook over boiling water until mixture forms crackling threads when a little is dropped into cold water, or until it reaches 280° to 285° on a candy thermometer. Quickly mix in nuts, orange peel, grated rind and flavoring.

Pour mixture into pan, to the depth of 1½ inches. Top with wafers or with another layer of sugar and waxed paper. Set in a cool, dry place (not the refrigerator) until firm. This can take from 30 minutes to 2 hours, depending on the humidity, and it can take as long as 7 hours, so plan accordingly. When firm, turn out of pans, remove paper if you used it, then cut into squares or rectangles, dust with confectioners' sugar and wrap each piece in waxed paper, foil or plastic wrap. Stored in an airtight container, this keeps for weeks.

Makes 1 to 1½ pounds

Variation: If you find it easier, you can mix stiffly beaten egg whites into hot honey right in the top of the double boiler. Stir caramelized sugar in after whites and then proceed. It is not necessary to work as quickly with this method, though the other produces a lighter result.

CHOCOLATE NOUGAT

Follow preceding recipe, eliminating flavorings and peel. Blend 2 cups unsweetened cocoa with 1½ tablespoons sugar and 3 tablespoons boiling water and stir into honey along with the nuts. Pour into pans, cool and cut as described.

SICILIAN TORRONE

[*Cubaica*]

Nothing could be more typically Sicilian or more Christmas-looking than this nougat rainbow. It is a veritable tutti-frutti mosaic, reminiscent of that other Sicilian dessert, the cassata. A word of caution: this is about the sweetest confection I've ever come across, one that might give you a toothache just looking at it.

(continued)

10 to 12 blanched toasted almonds
10 to 12 toasted hazelnuts, with skins rubbed off
½ cup shelled, unsalted pistachio nuts
⅓ cup candied red cherries
3 egg whites
9 cups confectioners' sugar, approximately
¼ cup unsalted butter, slightly softened
2 tablespoons almond extract
8 to 10 drops red food coloring
8 to 10 drops green food coloring
2 tablespoons cocoa
½ cup diced angelica or green candied cherries
Easiest Chocolate Icing, page 204 (optional)

Sliver almonds; cut hazelnuts in half; sliver or coarsely chop pistachio nuts; and cut red cherries in halves or quarters. Keep all separate from each other. Beat egg whites until foamy and combine with 7 cups of sugar, butter and almond extract. Mix thoroughly. Add enough additional sugar to make a paste that is just smooth enough to knead. Divide into 4 equal parts. Add red coloring to the first portion, green to the second, cocoa to the third and leave the fourth uncolored. Knead color into each portion until smoothly blended. Place a sheet of waxed paper on a long platter or a tray and sprinkle liberally with confectioners' sugar. Turn the green paste onto the platter in a layer about ½ inch thick and in a rectangle approximately 8 by 3 inches. Gently press green cherries, angelica or pistachio nuts into paste. Add layer of uncolored paste in same depth and dimensions and press almonds into it. Add the chocolate paste layer with hazelnuts, and top with the pink paste and red cherries. This particular arrangement is, of course, arbitrary, so feel free to express your own artistic yearnings in arranging the colored layers and adding any other candied fruits you like.

When all the paste is in place, press the sides in gently to form a loaf, with the top in a slight curve. Cover with waxed paper and chill for 24 hours. Peel off paper and coat sides and top with icing. Cool until icing hardens, then serve in slices. If you prefer to skip the icing, sprinkle the loaf with confectioners' sugar and serve sliced. Since it's so sweet, keep the slices thin and cut them again in halves. This will keep for weeks if it is well wrapped in foil or waxed paper and stored in an airtight container in a cool dry place.

Makes about sixteen ½-inch-thick whole slices.

COCONUT-WINE NOUGAT

[*Mexico, Chile and most of South America—Turron de Coco y Vino*]

- **⅔ cup strained orange juice**
- **2 cups sugar**
- **1 tablespoon light corn syrup or pure honey**
- **1 1-inch stick cinnamon**
- **½ pound grated unsweetened coconut (freshly prepared or packaged)**
- **4 egg yolks**
- **¼ cup red wine**
- **½ to ¾ pound Oblaten wafers, page 243**

Combine juice, sugar, corn syrup and cinnamon in a small, heavy-bottomed saucepan and boil for 5 minutes, or until mixture forms a thick syrup. Cook over low heat, stirring constantly until mixture is completely clear. Stir in coconut. Beat egg yolks until light and frothy. Spoon a little of the hot syrup into the eggs, beating constantly; then slowly pour this back into remaining hot syrup, beating constantly. Cook over low heat, stirring gently until mixture is thick and custard-like. Remove from heat and add wine. Cool completely and sandwich between small round or rectangular wafers. Place in a cool, dry corner for 2 or 3 hours, or until firm. Wrap each in foil, waxed paper or Saran.

Makes about 1 ½ pounds

SOUTH AMERICAN BISCUIT NOUGAT

[*Turron de Bizcocho*]

Follow preceding recipe, but crumble wafers and mix into candy instead of coconut. Line a pan or small carton with bakers' rice wafers (page 242), add candy, top with wafers and press lightly. Cool until firm; then cut into 1-inch squares.

PINOCCATE DI PERUGIA

[*Italy*]

½ pound pine nuts
1¼ cups sugar
¼ cup corn syrup
½ cup water
Grated rind of 1 lemon
2 tablespoons diced candied orange peel
1 teaspoon vanilla
Bakers' rice wafers, page 242 (optional)

Spread nuts in a single layer in a baking pan and dry out in a 275° oven for about 10 minutes. Combine sugar, corn syrup and water in a heavy-bottomed saucepan and cook over low heat, stirring constantly until sugar dissolves and liquid is clear. Cover pan and let cook for 4 or 5 minutes, or until sugar crystals melt down from sides of pan. Boil, without stirring, until mixture forms a medium hard ball when a little is dropped in cold water, or until it reaches 255° on a candy thermometer.

If mixture should crystallize, add more water to it and start over. Remove from heat, and with a wooden spoon, stir syrup against the sides of the pan until it becomes white and creamy. Quickly fold in nuts, grated rind, candied peel and vanilla. Spread quickly onto rounds of wafers or drop from a teaspoon onto buttered waxed paper or foil. Let dry until firm.

Makes about 1 pound

ORANGE GLAZED NUTS

[*United States*]

2 cups shelled hazelnuts, or shelled halves of walnuts, or pecans or blanched almonds
1⅔ cups sugar
½ cup orange juice
⅓ cup water

Toast shelled hazelnuts, walnuts or pecans in a 325° oven for about 10 minutes, or until golden brown. Place between two dishtowels and rub vigorously to remove skin. If you are using almonds, toast after blanching. Using a heavy-bottomed saucepan, cook sugar, orange juice and water over low heat until a little of the mixture forms a soft ball when dropped in cold water, or reaches 238° on a candy thermometer. Remove from heat and add nuts, stirring gently with a wooden spoon until syrup becomes dense and creamy and dull. Pour onto waxed paper and separate nuts quickly with a fork or tongs. Let dry on a rack until hardened.

Makes about 1 pound

PECAN BOURBON BALLS

[*Southern United States*]

- **1 cup confectioners' sugar**
- **2 tablespoons cocoa**
- **2½ cups crushed graham crackers**
- **1 tablespoon grated orange rind (optional)**
- **1½ cups chopped pecans**
- **2 tablespoons light corn syrup**
- **¼ cup bourbon**
- **Granulated sugar**

Sift sugar and cocoa and combine with wafers, orange rind and 1 cup nuts. Toss well to blend ingredients. Add corn syrup and bourbon and mix thoroughly. Shape into small balls, about 1 inch in diameter. Roll in granulated sugar and remaining nuts.

Makes about 2 dozen balls

PEPPERMINT CANDY CANES

[*North Europe and the United States*]

Christmas in the United States would hardly seem complete without red-and-white-striped peppermint candy canes. They are popular, too, throughout Northern Europe, most especially in Sweden, where they are called Polkagrisar. Having struggled to make these several times, I must say that I now consider candy canes the biggest bargain on the market. Do not attempt them unless you are experienced at candy-making or are willing to practice two or three times to perfect the technique. A candy thermometer and patience are essential; do not start unless you have both. And do not try to make more than the amount given here at one time.

3 cups sugar
1 cup water
1 tablespoon light corn syrup
2 teaspoons vinegar
Mineral oil
3 drops essence of peppermint
3 or 4 drops red food coloring
Confectioners' sugar
Cornstarch

Combine sugar, water, corn syrup and vinegar in a small heavy-bottomed saucepan. Place over low heat, stirring gently until sugar dissolves. Bring to a boil, cover pan and cook 2 to 4 minutes, or until all sugar crystals have melted down from the sides of the pan. Unmelted sugar will keep the canes from hardening. Uncover and continue at a low boil, without stirring, until mixture forms a hard ball when a little is dropped into ice water, or until it reaches 270° on a candy thermometer.

Grease a marble slab, a large baking pan or cookie sheet or a large platter with plenty of mineral oil. Carefully pour about two thirds of the mixture onto the oiled surface, leaving the remaining syrup in the pan on the warm stove (but not over a flame). Sprinkle peppermint onto the surface of the poured candy mixture, and with an oiled spatula, begin folding the mixture into the center from all sides, turning and folding until it becomes glassy and is cool enough to pick up. Oil your hands with mineral oil and stretch the cooled taffy, pulling it out slowly to about 14 inches in length and then folding it back on itself. Continue until candy is opaque, creamy and holds a shape at the ends. Do this in a fairly warm corner of the kitchen—near the stove or a radiator and away from open windows. Pull into long strips about ½ inch in diameter, and cut into desired lengths with a pair of oiled scissors. Add red coloring to remaining candy syrup, stir well and pour thin streams of red mixture on each side of each pulled candy strip. Twist together rope-fashion and form canes. Roll in a mixture of confectioners' sugar and cornstarch and let dry overnight. Shake off excess sugar and starch in the morning.

Makes about 1 pound

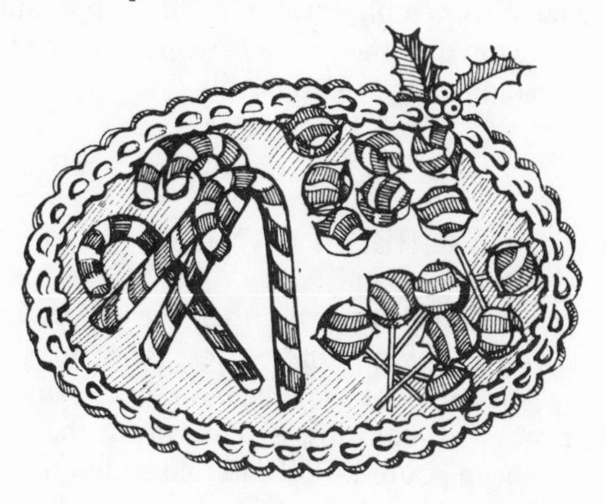

PEPPERMINT CUSHIONS

Follow preceding recipe, but twist red and white candy together and then cut diagonally and press gently into plump 1-inch squares.

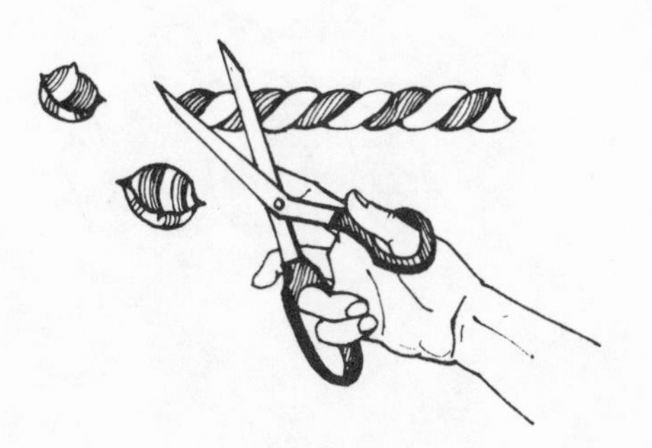

PEPPERMINT RINGS AND PRETZELS

Follow basic recipe, page 178, but twist red and white candy together and turn into ring or pretzel shapes.

CINNAMON OR CLOVE CANDY

Follow basic recipe, page 178, but substitute oil of cinnamon or oil of cloves (available from a pharmacy) for the peppermint essence. Leave candy white or color the entire batch red, which is especially suitable for cinnamon drops or squares.

RIBBON CANDY

This is even more difficult to make than the canes, and I would strongly advise you to buy it at the nearest candy store. However, if you are really game, here is the recipe, in theory anyway. Follow basic recipe, page 178, coloring and flavoring the entire candy batch when it has been poured. Pull and fold as described for canes. Stretch to thin bands about 1 to 1½ inches wide. Ripple these to form the ribbon effect.

Commercial ribbon candy usually has a striped effect, which is made by combining 2 layers of different-colored candy over each other before rippling, but if I were you I'd forget that step entirely. If you want an assortment of colors and flavors, prepare and shape each batch before starting the next.

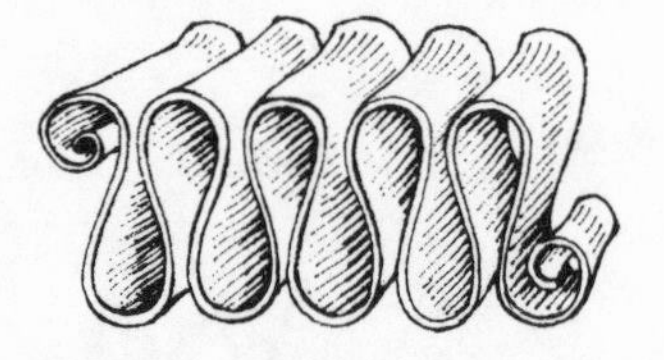

POPCORN BALLS

[*United States*]

This purely American confection can be served in bowls or can be hung by ribbons or wires from the Christmas tree.

Pour any of the hot syrups below over 8 cups of unseasoned, uncoated popped corn and toss gently with a wooden spoon until all kernels are coated. Let mixture become cool enough to handle. Butter hands lightly and pack popcorn gently into balls, snowball-fashion, making them any size you like.

Makes 14 to 16 small, or 8 to 10 large, balls.

White Popcorn Balls: Combine ¾ cup sugar, ⅔ cup water, 3 tablespoons white corn syrup and a pinch of salt and bring to a boil. Reduce heat and cook, covered, for 3 or 4 minutes, or until sugar crystals have melted from sides of pan. Continue cooking, uncovered and without stirring, until it reaches 290° on a candy thermometer, or when a little syrup dropped into cold water forms a crackling ribbon.

Golden Brown Popcorn Balls: Melt 2 tablespoons butter and stir in 1¾ cups brown sugar and 8 tablespoons water. When sugar dissolves, bring to a boil, reduce heat, cover and cook for 3 or 4 minutes, or until sugar has melted down from sides of pan. Uncover and cook without stirring until candy thermometer reaches 238°, or when a little syrup dropped in cold water forms a soft ball.

Honey Popcorn Balls: Cook ¾ cup honey, ¾ cup sugar and a pinch of salt over moderate heat until mixture reaches 245° on candy thermometer, or when a little of it dropped into cold water forms a soft ball.

QUINCE PASTE

The "golden apples" of Greek legend make this confection that is a Christmas standard throughout Europe and South America.

2 pounds quince
3 cups sugar, or as needed
Grated rind of 1 lemon
¼ teaspoon cinnamon
Confectioners' sugar

Cut unpeeled quince into eighths, lengthwise, and trim off core sections. Place in a large saucepan with ½ cup water and simmer, tightly covered, for 30 to 40 minutes, or until very soft. Allow to cool thoroughly in covered pan. Purée fruit through a food mill or sieve and then place in a heavy-bottomed saucepan with sugar. Simmer slowly, stirring almost constantly, until purée becomes very thick and leaves the sides of the pan. Fold in lemon rind and cinnamon. Spread or press mixture ½ inch thick in a baking pan or on a platter and let dry, uncovered, overnight, or for several days if necessary. Cut into rectangles or desired shapes with a cookie cutter, and turn pieces over so both sides dry. Dust with sugar and wrap each piece in waxed paper.

Makes about 2 pounds

To make a softer, more spreadable paste, cook mixture until thick but remove from heat before it is dry enough to leave the sides of the pan. Spread in pan as above and dry only until set. Store in jars.

South American and Spanish Membrillo: A piece of glass is placed over the platter or pan holding the quince paste, and it is set in the sun each day until dry.

German Quittenkonfekt: Add ½ cup finely crushed almonds, hazelnuts or pistachios to the cooked fruit paste.

Italian Cotognata: Flavor with a little lemon juice and brandy.

French Cotognac or Pâté de Coing: This is flavored with the juice and grated rind of an orange. It is especially popular in Provence, where it is always one of the thirteen sweets (along with assorted dried fruits and nuts) required for the Réveillon supper served after midnight mass on Christmas Eve.

APPLE CHEESE

[*England*]

Prepare apples instead of quince, following Quince Paste recipe, page 107. Use a little powdered cloves for flavoring. Cook pulp with sugar over low heat until mixture is clear and thick enough to form a sticky golden gum on the back of the mixing spoon. Store in well-covered jars. To serve most elegantly, turn out of jar onto a serving plate and garnish with unsweetened whipped cream and chopped hazelnuts or toasted almonds. Serve with unsweetened crackers.

SPICED ALMONDS

[*Canada, Europe, South America*]

- 2 cups confectioners' sugar
- 3 tablespoons cornstarch
- 1½ teaspoons cinnamon
- ⅓ teaspoon each powdered cloves, allspice, ginger and salt
- 2 egg whites
- 3 tablespoons white rum
- 2 cups blanched almonds

Sift together all dry ingredients. Beat egg whites with rum until frothy. Using a pair of tweezers or small tongs, dip each almond into egg white, letting excess drip off. Dredge almonds well with spice-sugar mixture, then place them ½ inch apart on an unbuttered cookie sheet. Toast in 300° oven for about 1 hour, or until golden brown and crisp. Cool thoroughly and store in an airtight container.

SNAPDRAGON

A Christmas custom from medieval England and meant for the intrepid . . . most effective in a darkened room. If you decide you like this little game and want to make it a tradition, you might look for an antique snapdragon platter, usually of Wedgwood with a holly-entwined border.

A handful of blanched almonds
3 or 4 large clusters of dark seedless raisins on branches
1 cup of brandy, or as needed

Place almonds and clusters of raisins on a heavy china platter. Heat brandy, pour over platter and ignite. Guests must snatch raisins and almonds one at a time from between flames. Dried prunes, apricots, figs or dates can be substituted for raisins, placing them in a mound in the center of the platter.

Sugarplums

Have you ever heard of a Sugar Plum Tree?
'Tis a marvel of great renown!
It blooms on the shore of the Lollipop sea
In the garden of Shut-Eye Town.
—Eugene Field

The original sugarplums were made in Portugal of fresh black figs or green plums, cooked and recooked for days on end in ever-thickening sugar syrups, to produce a sort of glacéed fruit. Prunes, figs, dates and other dried fruits are now prepared as sugarplums, and some of the variations follow. All can be wrapped in plain or colored foil, to be hung on the tree, or given as small gifts.

BYZANTINE SUGARPLUMS

- 3 pounds combined pitted dates, pulled figs, seeded raisins, currants
- ½ pound blanched walnuts or almonds
- ½ pound unsalted shelled pistachio nuts
- ½ pound crystallized ginger
- Grated rind of 2 oranges
- 3 tablespoons lemon juice or brandy, or as needed
- Confectioners' or granulated sugar

Chop combined fruits, nuts, ginger and rind through the coarsest blade of your meat grinder. Add just enough lemon juice or brandy to enable mixture to stick together. Shape into balls 1 to 1½ inches in diameter. Roll in sugar before wrapping. Vary assortment of fruits and nuts to suit your own taste, using any one or all of those suggested.

PORTUGUESE SUGARPLUMS

[*Bomboms de Figo*]

Prepare as in preceding recipe, using only ground soft dried figs and blanched toasted almonds and lemon juice if needed to moisten. Shape into balls 1 inch in diameter and roll in granulated sugar several times before wrapping.

PORTUGUESE CHOCOLATE AND ALMOND SUGARPLUMS

To make this version, you may use soft dried figs or steam the harder variety until they can be opened. Pull each fig open a little to create a pocket and stuff with a paste of grated dark semisweet chocolate and ground toasted almonds. These can be rolled in sugar and served cold, or they can be baked in a 275° oven for 5 to 10 minutes, turning once half through baking. Roll in sugar when cool.

STUFFED DRIED FRUITS

Steam whole dried apricots, prunes, dates or figs in a strainer over boiling water, about 10 minutes, or until soft. Remove pits carefully and refill cavities with marzipan, whole or chopped nut meats mixed with cinnamon and grated chocolate, or your favorite fondant. They may then be rolled in granulated or confectioners' sugar, or in colored sprinkles or grated coconut. Or dip them into a mixture of stiffly beaten meringue flavored with sugar and vanilla or almond extract, then dry on a rack set over a sheet of waxed paper. To make meringue for 2 pounds of fruit, beat 3 egg whites until stiff, gradually adding a pinch of salt and ¾ cup sugar and 1 teaspoon of extract flavoring.

GILDED WALNUTS

The most elaborate sugarplum variation I came across dates from nineteenth-century Czarist Russia and has nothing whatever to do with fruit.

Take the largest walnuts you can find, and without shelling them, dip each carefully in lightly beaten egg white and cover with gold leaf. Let dry on a rack and hang on the Christmas tree with gold threads or wires. You could do the same with silver leaf, of course, and there is no reason why you couldn't perform this shiny magic on pecans, hazelnuts or Brazil nuts if you can afford to.

TURKISH DELIGHT

[*Armenia—Lookoom*]

No Armenian Christmas table would be complete without a dish of Turkish Delight and another of sesame halvah. The recipe for the former is given herewith. As for the latter, it is the type of halvah found in New York and other large cities—and is never made in the home in either Armenia, or for that matter, Turkey, the country of its origin. I did call a Russian gentleman who, I was told, made his own sesame halvah. When I asked for the recipe, he answered, "But, my dear lady, I have never seen the cushions of your fingertips. How do I know if you can work the paste?" And so, dear reader, since I have never seen the cushions of your fingertips, it is probably safer to omit the recipe.

3 cups sugar
1½ cups water
3 tablespoons white corn syrup
3 envelopes unflavored gelatin
Juice of 1 lemon
¾ cup cornstarch
1 tablespoon rose water
¾ cup coarsely chopped pistachio nuts
Confectioners' sugar

Cook sugar with water and corn syrup in a heavy-bottomed saucepan until mixture forms a soft ball when a little is dropped in cold water, or reaches 240° on a candy thermometer. Keep hot. Soften gelatin in lemon juice. Dissolve cornstarch in ½ cup cold water and pour into hot syrup. Simmer slowly until very thick. Remove from heat, add gelatin and lemon juice and stir until gelatin dissolves. Stir in rose water and nuts. Sprinkle a thick layer of confectioners' sugar in an 8-inch square pan. Pour in candy and let set in a cool dry place (not the refrigerator) for 3 to 4 hours. Top with a layer of sugar and cut into 1-inch squares. Dredge lightly in additional sugar and store in an airtight container.

Makes about 5 dozen pieces

Variation: This candy can be colored with 2 or 3 drops of red or green food coloring, which is added to the mixture with rose water and nuts. It is not quite as customary for this to be done in Armenia as it is in Turkey.

DRINKS

Chapter Seven

ALABAMA HOT SCOTCH

Juice and rind of 1 lemon
¼ cup sugar
4 to 6 whole cloves
4 cups water
3 cups Scotch whiskey

Strain lemon juice and cut thin rind into fine slivers. Place in enameled saucepan with sugar, cloves and water. Bring to a boil, reduce heat and simmer 2 or 3 minutes. Add Scotch and bring to just below boiling point. Do not boil after Scotch has been added. Serve in heated mugs or glass punch cups.

About 6 servings

ATHOLE BROSE OR HOGMANAY

[*Scotland*]

Athole, a mountainous part of Scotland, is the birthplace of this brew (brose) that is served on New Year's Eve, or Hogmanay. It may be made with oatmeal water added to the ingredients below, but I think it would be preferable to most tastes without that.

1 cup honey (preferably heather honey from Scotland)
1½ to 2 cups heavy sweet cream
2 cups Scotch whiskey

Heat honey, and when it thins slightly, stir in cream. Heat together but do not boil. Remove from heat and slowly stir in whiskey. This may be served hot or thoroughly chilled. Makes 4 to 6 servings.

Variation: If you feel that you must try the oatmeal version, soak 1 cup oatmeal in 2 cups water overnight. Strain and mix liquid with other ingredients, to taste.

MEXICAN ATOLE OR CHAMPURRADO

There is undoubtedly a historic relationship between the preceding recipe and this cornmeal brew, which is drunk in Mexico during the Christmas season, when it is traditionally served with Mexican Kings' Cake, Rosca de Reyes, page 46.

½ cup masa flour (Mexican corn flour used for tamale dough and available packaged in Mexican neighborhoods and some supermarkets)
2 cups water
1 stick cinnamon
4 cups milk
2 cups brown sugar, firmly packed
3 ounces unsweetened chocolate

Stir masa into water, add cinnamon and cook over low heat, stirring frequently until thick. Add milk, sugar and chocolate and cook slowly, beating with a wire whisk until smooth and well blended. Bring to a boil once more and serve. To make a thicker, richer drink, beat 2 egg yolks with 3 tablespoons water and beat them into the hot chocolate just before serving. Heat, but do not boil after adding egg yolks.

Makes about 6 servings

SACK POSSET

Eggnog, originally a variation of the English Sack Posset, was made with milk and a strong ale and was usually served in a small mug called a noggin.

½ cup sugar
1 quart dry sherry
2 teaspoons nutmeg
18 eggs, well beaten
2 quarts milk or half-and-half (milk and cream)

Combine sugar, sherry and nutmeg in an enameled saucepan and heat thoroughly but do not boil. Stir frequently until sugar is completely dissolved. Remove from heat and cool. Beat eggs until thin and frothy; pour into sherry with milk and place over low heat, or in top of double boiler set over 1 inch of simmering water. Cook, stirring constantly until mixture coats a metal spoon. Serve hot or chilled, dusted with nutmeg.

Makes about 15 servings

PLANTATION EGGNOG

- **12 eggs, separated**
- **1 cup sugar**
- **2 cups rye or bourbon whiskey**
- **1 cup Jamaican rum**
- **4 cups half-and-half (milk and cream), or to taste**
- **1 cup heavy sweet cream, whipped**
- **Powdered nutmeg**

Beat yolks with ½ cup sugar until thick and very pale yellow. Beat in whiskey, rum and half-and-half. Beat egg whites, and as they begin to stiffen, gradually add remaining ½ cup sugar, beating well between additions. When whites are stiffly beaten, add to yolk mixture along with whipped cream. Fold together gently but thoroughly, using a rubber spatula. Serve from well-chilled punch bowl set in ice. Sprinkle with nutmeg.

Makes about 18 to 20 servings

TRADITIONAL ENGLISH EGGNOG

Follow preceding recipe, adding 1 extra cup half-and-half and ¼ cup brandy and substituting sherry or Madeira for the whiskey.

CHARLESTON ICE CREAM EGGNOG

- 12 eggs, separated
- 1 cup sugar
- 1 cup rye or bourbon whiskey
- ½ cup brandy
- 2 cups heavy cream, whipped
- 1 cup light cream
- 1 quart vanilla ice cream

Beat egg yolks with ½ cup sugar until thick and very pale yellow. Gradually stir in the whiskey and brandy, stirring well. Fold in the whipped cream, gently stir in the plain cream and finally fold in egg whites that have been stiffly beaten with balance of sugar. Just before serving, cut ice cream into pieces small enough to be ladled into punch cups and add to well-chilled punch bowl set in bed of ice.

Makes about 18 to 20 servings

COCONUT RUM EGGNOG

[*Latin America—Coquita*]

- 4 coconuts
- 4 small cans evaporated milk
- 12 eggs
- 4 small cans condensed milk
- 3 tablespoons vanilla, or to taste
- 3 to 4 cups white rum, to taste

Prepare coconut milk, using evaporated milk instead of water for liquid, according to instructions on page 242. Cool milk. Beat eggs thoroughly until light and frothy and combine with coconut milk, condensed milk, vanilla and rum. Beat well. Bottle and chill thoroughly. Since this is a thick and very rich drink, it is usually served in small liqueur-type glasses.

Makes about 14 servings

DUTCH OR ENGLISH BISHOP

1 unpeeled orange
12 to 18 whole cloves
Brown sugar
1 teaspoon cinnamon
Pinch of powdered cloves
Pinch of mace
½ teaspoon allspice
½ teaspoon powdered ginger, or 3 or 4 pieces cracked dried ginger
1 strip lemon peel
1 cup water
1 quart port wine
¼ cup brandy, heated
Nutmeg

Stud orange with whole cloves, pack thickly with brown sugar and roast in 350° oven until sugar caramelizes and forms a crust on the orange. Cut the orange in quarters and place it in a punch bowl. Meanwhile, simmer the remaining spices and lemon peel in water until water is reduced by half. Heat wine in an enameled saucepan until hot but not boiling. Combine spice syrup, wine and heated brandy in a punch bowl with the orange. Serve hot in punch cups sprinkled with nutmeg.

Makes about 8 to 10 servings

GLEE WINE

[*Germany and Scandinavia—Glühwein*]

Juice and rind of 2 lemons
2 cups water
8 to 10 whole cloves
1 2-inch stick cinnamon
3 tablespoons sugar
1 quart red Bordeaux-type wine

Strain lemon juice and cut the thin rind into fine slivers. Place in enameled saucepan with water, spices and sugar. Bring slowly to a boil, add wine and heat thoroughly but do not boil. Serve hot in heated punch cups.

Makes about 12 servings

MULLED CLARET

[*England*]

Follow preceding recipe, substituting oranges for lemons and adding 1 teaspoon grated nutmeg. For a stronger punch, add only 1½ cups boiling water and ¼ cup each orange liqueur and brandy to the hot punch before serving.

"Burnt" or flaming punches are a part of the New Year's Eve or Sylvester's Eve (Silvesterabend) celebration in Germany and Scandinavia.

SWEDISH GLÖGG

[*Julglögg*]

- **3 bottles red Bordeaux-type wine**
- **8 to 10 slices of orange, each studded with 4 or 5 cloves**
- **12 to 15 cardamom seeds**
- **2 bottles aquavit**
- **18 to 20 sugar cubes**
- **2 cups whole blanched almonds**
- **2 cups seedless raisins or currants**

Place wine in an enameled saucepan, add oranges with cloves and cardamom seeds and heat to boiling point. Cover tightly, remove from heat, and steep for 10 minutes. Heat aquavit in a separate enameled saucepan. Pour wine into thick ceramic or silver punch bowl and place a metal grate over bowl. Moisten sugar with a little aquavit and place on grate. Ignite remaining aquavit and keep pouring aquavit over sugar until all sugar has melted into wine. Place a few almonds and raisins in each punch cup and ladle hot liquid over them.

Makes about 36 to 40 servings

Variation: Use a half-and-half mixture of port wine and Bordeaux. Brandy can be substituted for aquavit. If you prefer, you can ignite soaked sugar in the bottom of the punch bowl, pour flaming aquavit over it and then extinguish with the seasoned hot wine. Chopped figs are often added with the raisins and almonds.

KRAMBAMBULI

[*Germany*]

2 bottles dry red or white wine
1 cup granulated sugar
1 pound cube sugar
½ cup dark rum or arrack, heated
1 bottle unchilled champagne

Heat the wine but do not boil. Pour into thick ceramic bowl and stir in granulated sugar until dissolved. Put a metal grate over the bowl and place cube sugar on the grate. Heat rum or arrack, ignite and pour while burning over sugar. When most of the sugar has melted into the wine, add champagne and ladle into punch cups.

Makes about 24 servings

FIRE TONG BOWL

[*Germany—Feuerzangenbowle*]

2 bottles dry red wine
1 cup granulated sugar
8 cloves
1 long strip of orange peel
2 slices lemon
Juice of 1 lemon
Juice of 1 orange
½ pound loaf sugar
1 cup rum, brandy or arrack, heated

Combine wine, granulated sugar, cloves, orange peel, lemon and fruit juices in an enameled saucepan and heat for 10 minutes but do not boil. Pour into a heated heavy punch bowl. Place a pair of fire tongs across the top of the bowl and on these set the loaf sugar moistened with some brandy or rum. Ignite remaining brandy or rum and pour flaming over sugar until all sugar has melted into the punch. If you cannot get loaf sugar, prepare this with cube sugar on a metal grate (see preceding recipe).

Makes about 15 punch-cup servings

JAMAICAN CHRISTMAS PUNCH

[*Sorrel*]

This bright red drink with its tart, refreshing flavor is among my favorite discoveries made while doing research for this book. It is based on a red flowering plant called sorrel in Jamaica, but which seems to be unlike the green leafy vegetable we know as sorrel or sour grass. The fresh or dried blossom is steeped in hot water to make this wonderful cold punch. Christmas aside, it would be a delightful and original drink to serve at a summer party here. Dried Jamaican sorrel can be purchased in West Indian and Latin-American grocery stores.

1 cup firmly packed dried Jamaican red sorrel blossoms
2-inch piece fresh ginger root, or 1 tablespoon cracked dried ginger
4 cups boiling water
¼ cup granulated sugar, or to taste
Quick-dissolving superfine granulated sugar
White Jamaican rum, to taste
Lime slices (optional)

Place sorrel blossoms in a pitcher or jar with the fresh or dried ginger. (Do not use powdered ginger as it will spoil the clarity and color of the drink.) Add boiling water and sugar and stir until sugar dissolves. Let stand until cool. Add some quick-dissolving sugar if more sweetening is needed, or add this when the drink is served. Strain and place in refrigerator overnight. To serve, fill 4 to 6 highball glasses with ice cubes, add chilled liquid and 1 to 2 jiggers white Jamaican rum, to taste. Garnish each glass with a slice of lime. This punch can be stored in the refrigerator for several days and used as needed.

Makes 4 to 6 servings

Variation: Though not authentically Jamaican, this drink would be beautiful served from a punch bowl. To do this, pour the chilled liquid over a large block of ice set in a punch bowl. Add lime slices and rum and sugar to taste. Ladle into chilled punch cups.

Makes 8 to 12 servings

SOUTH AMERICAN CHRISTMAS EVE PUNCH

[*Ponche de Nochebuena*]

8 cups water
16 cloves
1 cup seedless raisins
½ cup slivered blanched almonds
3 long cinnamon sticks
1 cup dark brown sugar, firmly packed
3 cups dark rum
2 tablespoons unsalted butter
8 thin orange slices, with peel
8 thin lemon slices, with peel
Extra cloves, optional

Boil water with cloves, raisins, almonds, cinnamon sticks and sugar for 20 minutes, or until mixture forms a thin syrup. Measure and add enough boiling water to make 6 cups. Pour into heated punch bowl, removing cinnamon sticks if you like. Add rum and butter. Stud fruit slices with a few additional cloves, if you wish, and add to punch. Serve hot in mugs or heated punch cups.

Makes about 16 servings

TOM AND JERRY

[*England and the United States*]

1 egg, separated
1 teaspoon maple sugar or granulated sugar
½ teaspoon allspice
1 ounce rum
½ ounce brandy
Hot milk, cream, half-and-half or boiling water
Nutmeg

Beat egg yolk with sugar until thick and pale yellow. Beat in allspice and rum. Beat egg white until stiff and fold into yolk mixture. Place egg mixture in a heated mug, add brandy and fill mug with hot milk, cream or boiling water. Dust with nutmeg.

Makes 1 drink

MEXICAN ROMPOPE

1 quart milk
1½ cups sugar
1 teaspoon vanilla extract, or
1 stick cinnamon
10 egg yolks
1 cup white rum

Bring milk to a boil, cool to lukewarm and add 1½ cups sugar. Bring to boil and simmer for 20 minutes. Add vanilla extract and cool. Beat egg yolks until very thick and ribbony. Gradually beat in milk and rum. Stir, strain and chill.

Makes about 15 servings

Wassails

A health to the King and Queene here.
Nexte crown the Bowle full
With gentle lamb's woll;
Add sugar, nutmeg and ginger,
With store of ale too;
And this ye must do
To make the wassail a swinger.
Robert Herrick

Swinging or otherwise, spiced ale has been a part of the English Christmas since medieval times; its name derived from the Anglo-Saxon "was hal," meaning "be hale." Not originally a serving bowl, the wassail was a large drinking cup passed around to the assembled guests. Those who could not afford to make their own wassail carried wooden bowls through the streets while singing Christmas carols—going a'wassailing—in hopes of receiving some of the warming brew. This combination of spiced ale and roasted crab apples was also known as lamb's wool and church ale, the latter referring to the church custom of selling this drink around Christmas to raise alms for the poor. The toast that flavors the wassail was considered a choice morsel and everyone wanted to be lucky enough to "drink a toast."

A SWINGING WASSAIL

1 quart ale
1 teaspoon cinnamon
5 or 6 pieces cracked ginger or 1 teaspoon powdered ginger
2 cups sherry wine
Juice and thinly pared rind of 1 lemon
Sugar, to taste
2 slices toasted bread
6 or 8 roasted crab apples or 2 or 3 roasted large apples

Heat ale in an enameled saucepan until it is just below the boiling point. Stir in spices, sherry, lemon juice, slivered rind and sugar. Stir until sugar dissolves, then cover and steep over low heat for 20 to 30 minutes. Do not boil at any time. Pour into heated punch bowl. Add toast and apples. Ladle into warm punch cups. Makes about 12 servings.

Variation: Twelve well-beaten eggs may be beaten into the hot wassail before the apples are added. An eighteenth-century version of this recipe calls for brown sugar instead of white, beer rather than ale. The cooled drink, toast and all, may be bottled and chilled for several days, then poured into the wassail bowl and garnished with hot roasted apples.

CIDER WASSAIL

For a non-alcoholic version of the preceding recipe, substitute sweet apple cider for the ale and sherry.

ENGLISH FARMERS' WASSAIL

Follow recipe for A Swinging Wassail (above), but substitute hard cider for ale and 1 cup dark rum for sherry.

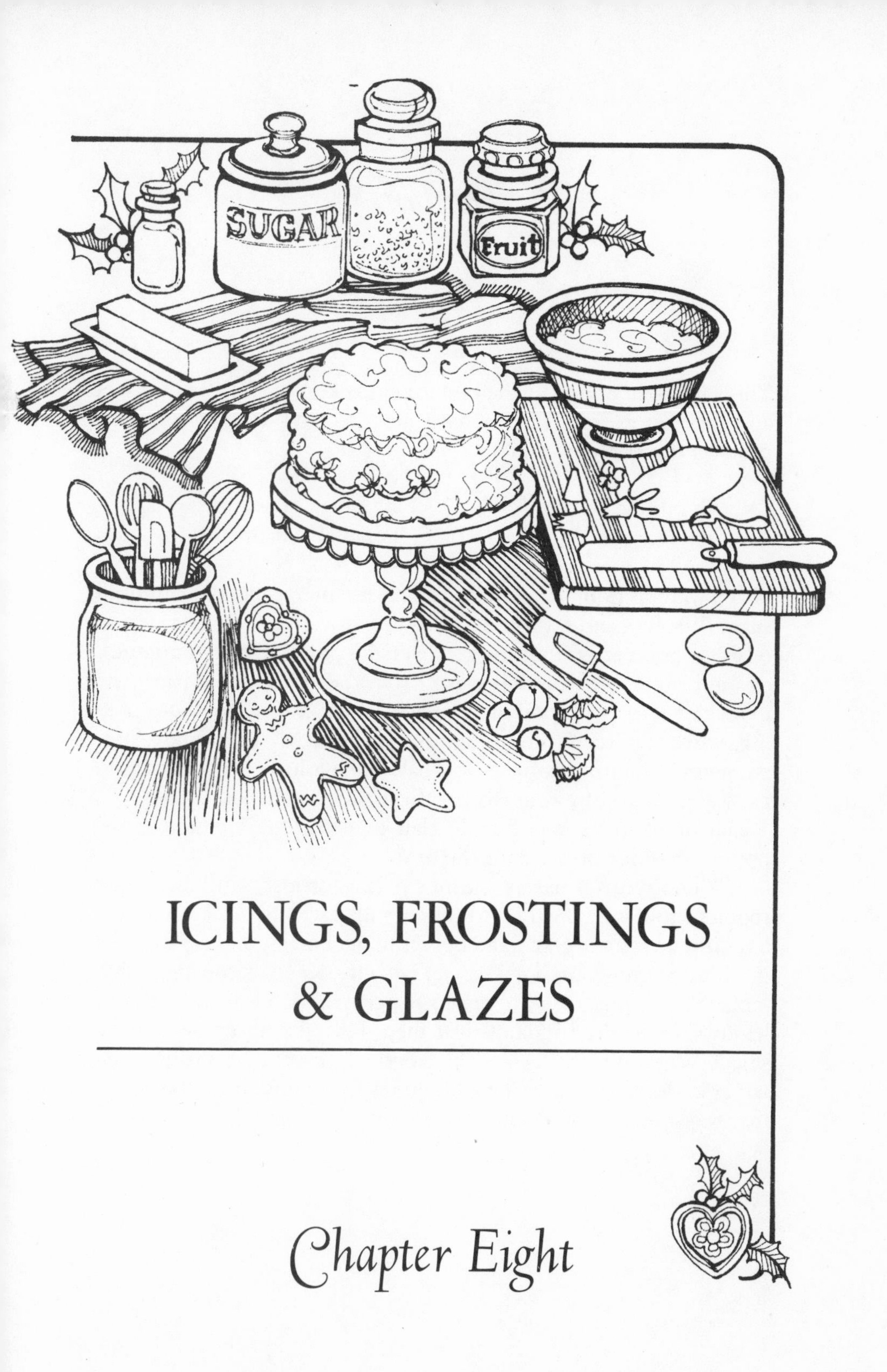

ICINGS, FROSTINGS & GLAZES

Chapter Eight

Fondant

This icing is far and away the best for any cakes, cookies, petits fours and candies, as it retains its hard gloss, is slow to melt and also protects the cake or candy.

¾ cup boiling water
2¾ cups sugar
Tiny pinch cream of tartar (about 1/16 teaspoon)

When water is boiling, stir in sugar and remove from heat. Stir until sugar dissolves and return to low heat. Stir in cream of tartar vigorously to prevent boiling over. Cover the pan for 5 or 6 minutes, or until sugar crystals melt down from the sides of the pan. Any unmelted sugar will spoil the fondant. Uncover and continue cooking, without stirring, until mixture reaches 238° on a candy thermometer, or until it forms a soft ball when a little is dropped into ice water. Carefully remove pan from stove and pour syrup to a 1-inch depth on a wet marble slab or a platter. Do not scrape bottom or sides of pan into mixture.

When syrup is barely warm, stir it vigorously with a wooden spoon or fold it from edges to center with a wide spatula. Continue until it is no longer glassy and begins to get creamy and stiff. Knead it, a little at a time, until it is soft and pliable. Keep unkneaded batch moist by covering it with waxed paper or a damp towel. If your hands stick to the fondant, dust them lightly with confectioners' sugar. When fondant is well kneaded, store it in an airtight container in the refrigerator for 24 hours before using. It can be stored that way for several weeks.

Makes about 4 cups

FONDANT ICING

Place 1½ cups basic fondant mixture (see above) in a double boiler set over 1 inch of boiling water. Add 1½ tablespoons liquid made up of hot water and any flavoring you want to use—vanilla or almond extract, peppermint essence, lemon juice, rum, brandy, orange juice or brewed coffee. Food coloring may also be added. Stir with a wooden spoon as fondant melts. Heat and thin more if necessary until fondant will pour easily and smoothly but is still thick enough to mask the cake. Place cake or cookies to be iced on a rack and pour fondant over them, rotating them so icing spreads evenly. If it stiffens before you have used all of it, reheat and use.

Makes enough to ice top and sides of two 9-inch layer cakes

CHOCOLATE FONDANT ICING

Add ½ tablespoon water and 1 ounce melted bitter or semisweet chocolate to fondant as it is warming. Use for Lebkuchen, Neapolitan Mustaches, Norwegian and English Yule Logs, Sicilian Torrone, and as called for in various other recipes.

EASIER CHOCOLATE FONDANT ICING

⅓ cup corn syrup
1 cup plus 2 tablespoons sugar
½ cup hot water
3 cups sifted confectioners' sugar
1 tablespoon lightly beaten egg white
2 teaspoons glycerin or mild-flavored oil
2 ounces bitter chocolate, melted

Combine syrup, sugar and water and cook over low heat, stirring constantly until sugar is completely dissolved and mixture is as crystal-clear as the corn syrup was. This will take about 10 minutes. Cover the pan and continue cooking for 6 or 7 minutes, or until all sugar crystals melt down from sides of pan. Uncover and boil mixture rapidly, without stirring, for 5 minutes. Cool completely.

Gradually sift confectioners' sugar into syrup until mixture is a very thick paste. Place over simmering water and beat with a wooden spoon until barely tepid. Beat in egg white, glycerin or oil and melted chocolate. This mixture can be thickened with a little more confectioners' sugar or thinned with a spoonful or two of water. Pour over cake. Small cakes such as Lebkuchen can be held with tongs and dipped in glaze and then put on rack to dry, if you want all sides covered.

Makes enough for top and sides of two 9-inch cakes

Variation: Instead of chocolate, this can be flavored with vanilla, almond or lemon extract, rum, brandy or strongly brewed black coffee, to taste. If you do not make the icing chocolate, you may add a few drops of food color to mixture, along with the flavoring, or leave it white.

EASIEST CHOCOLATE ICING

Although not as hard or long-lasting as the preceding fondants, this icing is made by a very simple and almost foolproof method.

⅔ cup sugar
5 tablespoons water
3 ounces semisweet chocolate
1 teaspoon vanilla

Cook sugar and water over low heat until sugar dissolves. Boil rapidly until syrup spins a thread when the spoon is taken out of it, or until it reaches 234° on a candy thermometer. Stir in chocolate and beat until melted. Stir in vanilla and spread or pour over cake or cookies.

Makes enough for top and sides of a 9-inch layer cake

CREAMY CHOCOLATE ICING

3 ounces bitter chocolate
3 tablespoons unsalted butter
¼ cup hot scalded milk
2½ cups sifted confectioners' sugar
Pinch of salt
½ teaspoon rum flavoring, or 1 tablespoon vanilla extract

Melt chocolate and butter in the top of a double boiler over boiling water. Combine hot milk, sugar and salt and beat into chocolate mixture. Add flavoring and continue beating until thin enough for dipping and pouring. Use while hot.

Makes enough for one 8- or 9-inch layer cake

CREAMY SUGAR GLAZE

Perfect for coffeecake and Christmas cookies.

2 cups sifted confectioners' sugar
½ teaspoon vanilla or almond extract, or 1 teaspoon rum or brandy
½ cup milk or heavy sweet cream, approximately, as needed

Resift sugar into a bowl and mix in flavoring. Heat milk or cream and gradually stir into sugar, mixing well until you have the right consistency. You may use a fairly thick mixture of this that can be spread onto cookies with a knife, or a thinner mixture that can be poured over coffeecakes. Decorate with cherries and nut meats and candied fruits or sugar sprinkles (page 244).

Makes enough to ice a 10-inch round coffeecake

Variation: A few drops of food coloring may be added to this.

WHITE SUGAR GLAZE

For cookies and cakes, and especially for Lebkuchen, pages 89–90, and Baseler and Berner Leckerli, pages 104–105.

⅓ cup confectioners' sugar
1½ tablespoons cornstarch
½ teaspoon vanilla or almond extract
1 teaspoon rum or brandy (optional)
½ to 1¼ tablespoons hot water, or as needed

Combine sugar, cornstarch, flavorings and rum or brandy. Gradually stir in hot water, a tablespoonful at a time, until you have a smooth thick paste. Spread on warm cookies. If mixture cools and thickens as you work, thin with additional hot water. Sugar sprinkles can be scattered on the glaze before it hardens.

Makes ¼ cup, or enough to ice about fifteen 1½-inch cookies

ALMOND PASTE ICING

1 cup confectioners' sugar
1 cup fine quick-dissolving granulated sugar
2 cups blanched whole almonds, finely ground
3 egg yolks, beaten
1 teaspoon lemon juice or rose water
½ teaspoon almond extract

Sift sugars together and toss with ground almonds. Beat egg yolks with flavorings and stir into dry ingredients, adding more confectioners' sugar if needed to make a dough smooth enough to be kneaded. Add lemon juice if it is crumbly. Knead until smooth on a board sprinkled with confectioners' sugar. Roll thinly between sheets of waxed paper and cut to fit cake. Instructions for applying to cake follow Royal Icing recipe, below.

Makes enough to cover 1 large fruit cake

ROYAL ICING

3 egg whites
Pinch of salt
3½ to 4 cups confectioners' sugar
1 teaspoon lemon juice
1 teaspoon glycerin
Food coloring (optional)

Beat egg whites, salt, 3 cups sugar, lemon juice and glycerin until mixture stands in stiff peaks. Add more sugar only if necessary to make the paste stiff. Mix in food coloring, dividing batch in portions beforehand if you want more than one color. Spread on cake in thin layers, letting each dry before adding the next.

Makes 2 cups, or enough for top and sides of 8-inch cake

To Apply Almond Paste and Royal Icings: These are usually applied together, especially on fruit cakes. However, the same rules pertain whether they are used separately or together, as on the Norwegian and English Yule logs. The cake should be cool, and it is a good idea to brush the surface of it with a little warm melted jam (apricot or raspberry, or orange marmalade) or lightly beaten egg white. Roll paste as directed in preceding recipe. After placing cut paste on cake, press into place gently and store for a day or two before icing. The Royal Icing should be spread in thin layers, as described above. Smooth top layer of icing with warm blade of a spatula and decorate as desired. These icings, used in combination, keep cakes sealed and fresh for months or even years.

DECORATIVE SUGAR ICING

This is used for various cookies, the Gingerbread House, page 223, Lucia Ginger Snaps, page 110, the Gingerbread Men, page 109, and Bread Dolls, page 21. Prepare Royal Icing (above), eliminating glycerin. When whites are beaten into stiff shiny peaks, divide and color each portion as you wish. Half fill a pastry tube fitted with a narrow tube and pipe design onto cookie or cake, holding tip of tube 2 to 3 inches from surface of cookie. Or spread icing with a knife to cover large areas like the roof of the gingerbread house or the complete surface of cookies. This hardens quickly, so if you want to top the icing with colored sugar or sprinkles, do so at once.

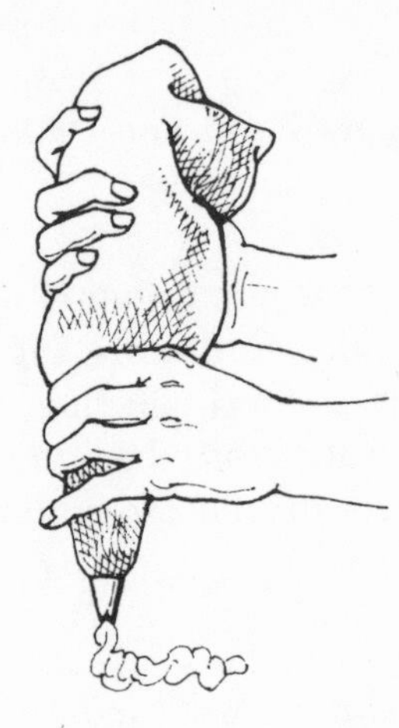

GOLDEN ALMOND ICING

For pound cakes, white or light fruit cakes and especially for English Twelfth Cake, page 56.

⅔ cup ground blanched almonds
½ cup sugar
¼ cup unsalted butter, softened
¼ cup white rum
2 egg yolks
1 or 2 drops almond extract

Combine all ingredients and beat vigorously with a wooden spoon until mixture is creamy, pale yellow and soft. Spread over cooled cake with a spatula. Let harden in a cool dry corner several hours or overnight.

Makes 1½ cups, or enough to ice a 7-to-8-inch cake

MERINGUE SNOW FROSTING

A snowy frosting for cookies, especially for Sugar Drops, page 120.

2 egg whites
2¾ cups confectioners' sugar
Few drops of vanilla or almond extract
¾ cup chopped blanched almonds

Beat egg whites until they become foamy. Gradually beat in sugar and flavoring until whites stand in stiff shiny peaks. Stir in almonds. Spread on cookies and decorate with candied fruit peel, candied cherries, nut meats or colored sugar or sprinkles.

Makes enough for about 7 dozen cookies

HONEY SYRUP GLAZE

This syrup is used with almost all of the fried Christmas pastries in Chapter Four. Flavoring variations are noted in individual recipes.

1½ cups honey
1 tablespoon cinnamon or 1 2-inch stick cinnamon
1 to 2 tablespoons lemon juice

Bring honey to a boil with all ingredients. Simmer for a minute or two, remove stick of cinnamon if you have used it, and pour over pastry or use for dipping.

Makes about 1½ cups syrup

HARD SAUCE

To be served with plum puddings or fruit cakes.

- 1 cup (½ pound) unsalted butter
- 1¾ cups confectioners' sugar
- Rum or brandy, as needed
- Confectioners' sugar and nutmeg, for sprinkling (optional)

Cream butter with sugar, adding a little extra sugar if needed to make a stiff paste. Gradually beat in as much rum or brandy as the mixture can absorb while still remaining stiff. Place in glass or china serving dish or jar. Cover and store in the refrigerator. Sprinkle with sugar and nutmeg before serving.

Makes about 2 cups

Variation: Spices such as cinnamon, nutmeg and cloves can be beaten in with the butter and sugar, to taste. Two cups brown sugar, firmly packed, may be substituted for the confectioners' sugar, in which case add 2 or 3 tablespoons cream with the rum or brandy.

HOT OR COLD WINE SAUCE

For plum puddings.

- 2 egg yolks
- 1 whole egg
- ½ cup plus 1 tablespoon sugar
- 1 teaspoon cornstarch
- 1 cup dry sherry or Madeira
- 1 teaspoon lemon juice
- 2 egg whites, stiffly beaten

Combine egg yolks and whole egg in the top of an enameled double boiler. Add sugar and cornstarch and beat until light and frothy. Gradually beat in wine and lemon juice. Set over 1 inch of simmering water. Cook and beat constantly until mixture is thick enough to coat a metal spoon. Remove pan from hot water and beat in egg whites gradually. This may now be served hot. If you want to use it cold, place pot in a bowl of ice and continue beating until mixture is cold and thick.

Makes about 2 cups, or 4 to 8 portions

SHAKER EXCELLENT PUDDING SAUCE

From *The Shaker Cookbook,* by Caroline B. Piercy.

2 cups brown or maple sugar
2 tablespoons cornstarch
½ teaspoon salt
2 cups boiling water
2 tablespoons unsalted butter
2 tablespoons vinegar
1 teaspoon vanilla
Pinch of nutmeg

Mix sugar, cornstarch and salt; add boiling water and boil 5 minutes, stirring frequently. Then add remaining ingredients and blend. Serve very hot over steamed pudding.

VANILLA SUGAR

Place 1 pound confectioners' or granulated sugar in a jar with 2 or 3 vanilla beans. Close jar tightly and let stand for 48 hours before using. Replenish sugar as it is used up. Use as called for in individual recipes. Beans need replacing only after 4 or 5 months.

CINNAMON SUGAR

Mix 1½ to 2 tablespoons cinnamon into 1 cup granulated or confectioners' sugar. Store in shaker or jar.

FRIENDS BEARING GIFTS

Chapter Nine

With giving and sharing being the very essence of the Christmas spirit, it seems particularly appropriate to have this new addition to this book. All the recipes in this chapter are Christmas favorites of friends.

With few exceptions, all these recipes are childhood favorites with strong ethnic, regional, and traditional origins, and each bears the unique style of the person who contributed it.

The generosity of these contributors has greatly enriched this book and added much to the general knowledge of the traditional sweets of this season.

Totally irresistible pastries, cakes, tarts, cookies, and croissants are the stock-in-trade of the bright and charming Bonté Patisserie on Third Avenue in New York. The jovial and generous Norman proprietor is Maurice Bonté, the accomplished pâtissier *who oversees the bake shop. The Three Kings' Cake below, with its buttery, flaky pastry and fragrant almond filling, is made with Mr. Bonté's simplified puff pastry that lends itself to any traditional uses for that flaky crust.*

GALETTE DES ROIS

PUFF PASTRY:

2½ cups (1¼ pounds) unsalted butter
2⅓ cups cake flour
2 cups unbleached all-purpose flour
1¼ cups ice water
2 teaspoons salt

EGG WASH:

1 egg lightly beaten with 1 tablespoon water

Cut butter into flour, using two knives, until butter-flour clumps are roughly the size of hazelnuts. Flour should not be totally blended with butter. Pour ice water into the bowl of an electric mixer and add salt. (If you do not have an electric mixer with a flat beater, see note below.) Put flour and butter mixture on top of the water. Turn mixer on low speed and, using the flat beater, mix for 1 to 2 minutes, until dough forms a ball that still has heavy streaks of butter. Flatten ball, patting it into a rectangle. Cover with plastic wrap and let it rest for 10 minutes in the refrigerator.

On a lightly floured board, using a lightly floured rolling pin, roll dough to a rectangle that is ½ inch thick and about 10 by 16 inches. Fold in three as shown. Turn over and roll again to ½ inch thickness. Fold dough into four parts, first by folding in half vertically, then again in half horizontally. Wrap in plastic and chill 30 minutes. Turn dough over and roll out to ½ inch thickness, into a rectangle measuring about 12 inches by 18 inches. Fold in four again, making a packet that is about 1½ inches thick. Wrap in plastic and chill 30 minutes or overnight. It is now ready to be rolled out into its final shape for baking.

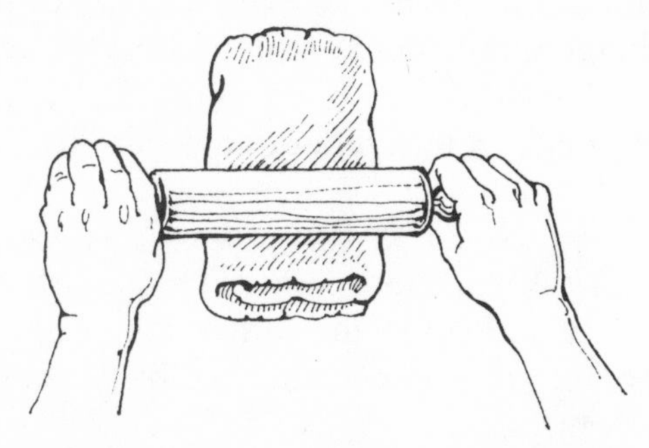

To shape the galette: Cut chilled dough into 2 squares, each weighing about 12 to 14 ounces. Roll each piece into a square that is about ½ inch thick.

Turn the four corners of each square of rolled dough into the center so the points meet but do not overlap. Gently pushing the dough with the edge of your hand, shape it roughly into a circle. Pat the top smooth as you work.

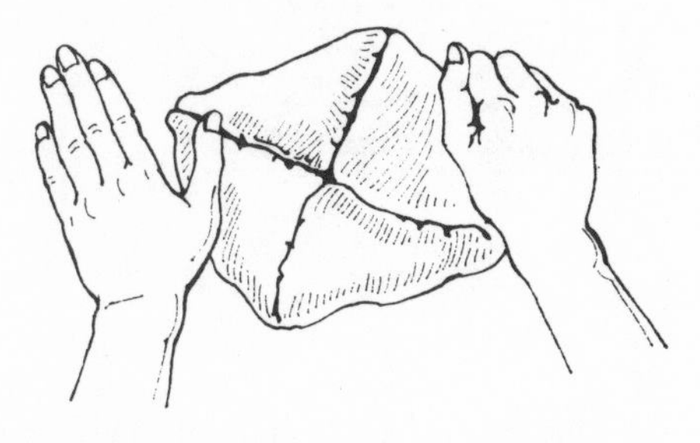

Let each piece of dough rest in the refrigerator for 20 minutes. Do not wrap in plastic. Then, with a rolling pin, roll each piece to a circle that is 11 to 12 inches across, and about ¼ inch thick. Lay a sheet of unbuttered baker's parchment on a heavy cookie sheet (or two stacked cookie sheets if yours are light aluminum) and lay one circle of dough on the sheet.

Lightly moisten a 1-inch band around the rim of the circle of dough on the parchment. Cover center with a layer of almond cream mixture (see below) that is about ¼ inch thick. Spread filling, leaving a ¾-inch margin around the rim of the dough circle. Use about 1½ cups of the almond filling. Cover with remaining circle of dough and seal the edges of the dough by pressing down with your finger just a little inside the extreme edge of the dough. The edge of the dough should not be sealed. Press about ½ inch in from the edge.

Rest the galette in refrigerator anywhere from 15 minutes to 12 hours or overnight.

Preheat oven to 425° F. Brush dough with egg wash.

Using a very sharp, finely pointed knife, slash the edges of the dough diagonally and cut in the rest of the design as shown. Cut just deeply enough to break the surface of the dough but do not cut all the way through.

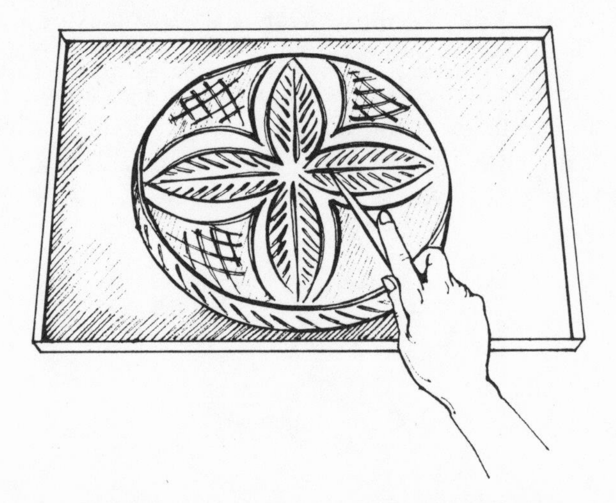

Bake in middle of oven for 10 minutes, then lower heat to 375°F. and continue baking for 30 minutes. The crust should be a rich golden brown and firm when gently pressed.

As soon as galette is removed from oven, brush top with Vanilla Sugar Syrup (see below). Cool several hours before serving.

ALMOND CREAM FILLING

½ cup (¼ pound) unsalted butter
½ cup fine granulated sugar
3 eggs, lightly beaten
½ cup almond flour, sifted (page 242)
2 tablespoons all-purpose flour
2 tablespoons rum or 1 teaspoon vanilla

Using an electric mixer at medium speed, cream butter and sugar together until light and fluffy. Add beaten egg gradually, beating well between additions until all has been beaten in. Stop the mixer. Add both flours to the bowl, mixing in gently but thoroughly with a wooden spoon. Then stir in rum or vanilla. Spread on puff pastry as directed.

VANILLA SUGAR SYRUP

½ cup granulated sugar
3 tablespoons water
1 teaspoon vanilla

Combine sugar and water and cook until clear and syrupy—about 8 minutes. Stir in vanilla. Let cool slightly, but brush on while still warm.

Note: The puff pastry for the galette can be made without an electric mixer. To make the dough by hand, work on a pastry board and cut butter into flour, using two knives, until it is roughly blended. When butter-flour clumps are the size of hazelnuts, shape into a mound and make a well in the middle. Add salt and water to well and work flour-butter mixture into water with the fingers, working lightly till blended. Do not overmix. When mixture can form a ball but still shows clear streaks of butter, flatten the ball, patting it into a rectangle, cover with plastic wrap and refrigerate for 10 minutes. Proceed with rolling and shaping according to directions above.

A professional chef and baker, John Clancy teaches an extraordinary class in baking as well as several on special aspects of cooking. The author of Oven Cookery *and* The John Clancy Baking Book, and the proprietor of a restaurant that bears his name, *Mr. Clancy found this Christmas recipe in an obscure German cookbook, and perfected it. It is reminiscent of the Advent Pretzel, page 18.*

STAR OF ZURICH

1 pound unbaked puff pastry (page 220)
1 egg white, lightly beaten with a fork
1 egg yolk, lightly beaten
3 egg whites
⅓ cup granulated sugar
½ cup blanched, toasted, and ground almonds
½ cup grated, unsweetened coconut
Confectioners' sugar, whipped cream, candied cherries and angelica (optional) for garnish

Using parchment, form a star as described below.

Roll out folded and chilled puff pastry to approximately ¼ inch thickness. Place on a large, heavy, unbuttered cookie sheet.

Using the paper pattern, cut out the star. From trimmings, cut ½-inch-wide strips.

Brush the edges of the star with beaten egg white. Place strips on the edges of the star and brush them with egg yolk. Let pastry rest in refrigerator for at least 3 and preferably 4 hours.

Preheat oven to 425°F.

Beat the 3 egg whites to soft peaks. Add the sugar gradually and continue beating until the whites are firm but still shiny. Fold in the almonds and the coconut.

Fill center of puff pastry star with the nut and coconut meringue. Be sure to extend the filling to the points of the star and to mound it toward the center of the star.

Bake for about 30 minutes or until the pastry has risen and is golden brown.

Cool thoroughly and garnish with a sprinkling of confectioners' sugar and lightly sweetened whipped cream piped around the edges of the pastry. Candied cherries and angelica may also be added for decoration.

Makes 6 to 8 servings

To Make a Star Pattern Baker's parchment or any stiff, clean paper can be used for this. Cut two 12-inch squares from the paper. Cut each in half diagonally, forming two triangles on rolled-out pastry that has been laid onto the baking sheet. Discard one triangle. Arrange the triangles as shown in the accompanying diagram. Cut around the template with a thin, sharp knife to make a dough star.

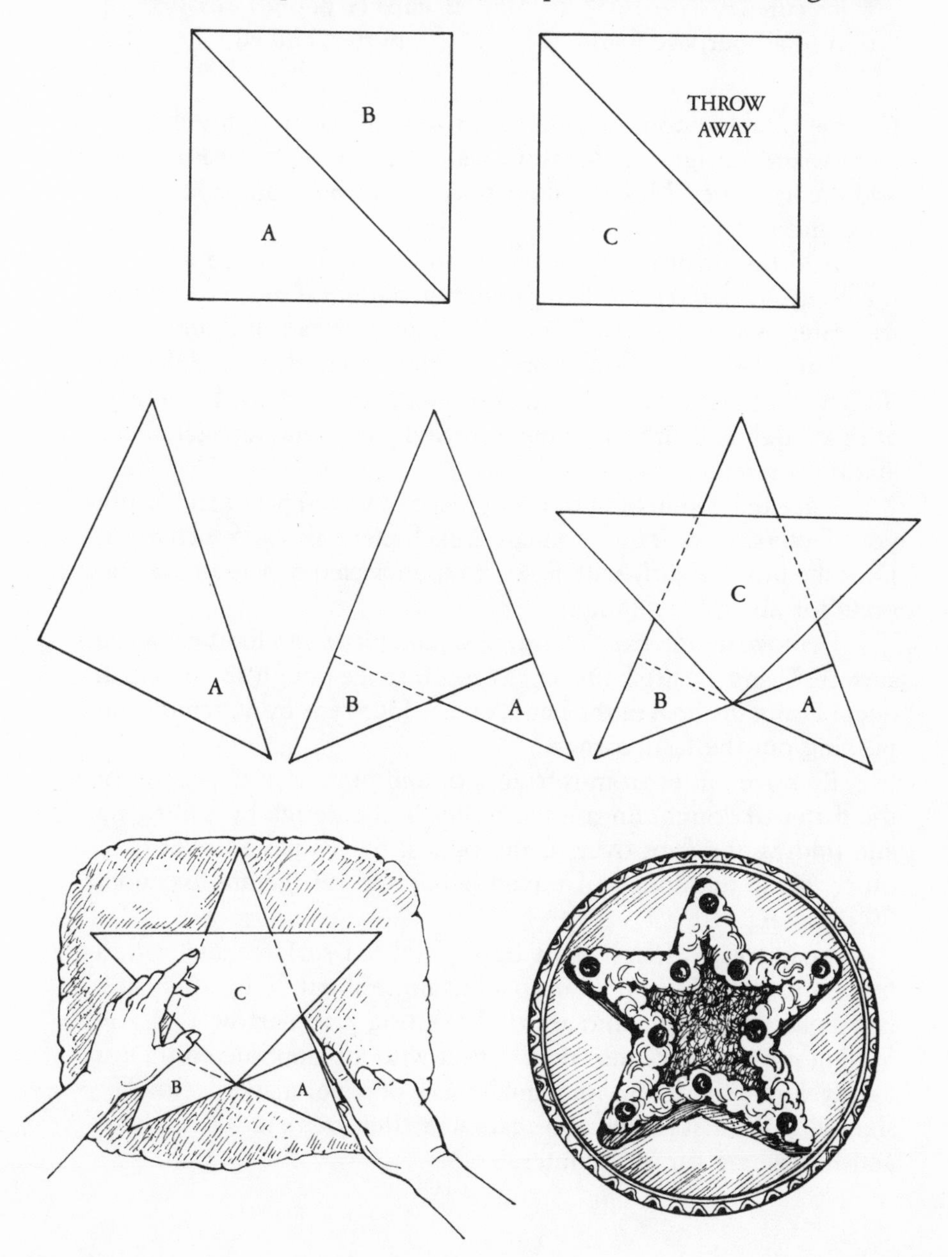

PUFF PASTRY

- 6 tablespoons unsalted butter
- 1½ cups water
- 4 ice cubes
- 6 cups all-purpose flour
- ½ teaspoon lemon juice
- 1½ teaspoons salt
- 2 cups (1 pound) unsalted butter, chilled

Cut the 6 tablespoons of butter into small pieces roughly the size of peas and refrigerate. Measure water in a two-cup measure and add the ice cubes. Measure flour into a large bowl and add lemon juice and salt.

Add the small pieces of butter and 1 cup of the ice water to the flour. Work the ingredients together, adding as much additional ice water as necessary to form a medium-firm ball of dough.

Turn the ball of dough onto a lightly floured surface. Knead dough until butter is well incorporated, about 3 to 4 minutes. Sprinkle lightly with flour, wrap in waxed paper, and refrigerate for about 30 minutes.

Place the pound of butter on a piece of waxed paper and, using your fingers, work it into a square 6-inch piece about ½ inch thick. Dust the butter lightly with flour, wrap in waxed paper, and refrigerate for about 20 minutes.

Remove dough from refrigerator and place on a lightly floured surface. Using a sharp knife, cut a cross into the dough about ¾ inch deep. Using the heel of the hand, create four flaps by flattening and pushing out the four corners.

Remove butter from refrigerator and place it in the center of the flattened dough. Encase the butter in the dough by pulling up and folding the flaps over it, the opposite flaps placed over each other. Wrap the dough in waxed paper and refrigerate for about 20 minutes.

Again place dough on a lightly floured surface, and with a floured rolling pin, roll it out to a rectangle about 10 by 20 inches.

Fold the dough into thirds by lifting one narrow end and folding it over the center, then repeat with the opposite end. Dust lightly with flour. Top with a small piece of paper marked with "1" signifying the first rolling and again wrap the dough in waxed paper and refrigerate for 20 minutes.

Place chilled dough vertically on a floured surface, one narrow open end facing you. With a rolling pin, roll the pastry with a firm and even pressure into a rectangle 10 by 20 inches. Again fold it into thirds, note that it has been rolled twice, and chill for 20 minutes.

Roll out and chill the dough three more times. The pastry should have a total of five rollings. If butter breaks through, sprinkle the butter spot heavily with flour.

Note: One-half of this recipe is sufficient for the Star of Zurich cake. The remainder may be frozen for future use.

ROTOLO DI NATALE

Giuliano Bugialli, a native of Tuscany, is especially interested in the medieval foods of that north Italian region. In his excellent cooking school, as well as in his book *The Fine Art of Italian Cooking,* he adapts antique recipes such as the one below so that they can be made with modern ingredients and with modern equipment. The sharp contrasts of chocolate and citrus rind, nuts and raisins make this lusty rolled yeast cake especially festive for Christmas breakfast. Mr. Bugialli feels that the proper flavor and texture depend upon the use of fresh yeast in cake form. It is possible, however, to come close using four 1-ounce packages of powdered yeast.

- 4 ounces cake yeast (or 4 tablespoons dry yeast)
- 2 cups lukewarm milk
- 3⅓ cups unbleached flour
- 1¾ cups raisins
- ½ pound shelled walnuts, coarsely chopped
- ¼ pound pignoli nuts
- 1 cup granulated sugar
- Grated rind of 2 oranges
- Grated rind of 2 lemons
- 5 tablespoons unsweetened cocoa powder
- ½ cup plus 2 tablespoons unsalted butter
- 2 eggs, separated
- ½ cup dark rum
- Pinch of salt

Mash the yeast and mix with 1 cup lukewarm milk. Place flour in a large bowl and make a well. Pour dissolved yeast into the well and mix with a wooden spoon until about one-fourth of the flour is incorporated into the liquid. Cover the bowl with a cotton dish towel and let stand in a warm, draft-free corner for about 1 hour or until the sponge has doubled in bulk.

While the dough rises, prepare filling. Soak raisins in the remaining 1 cup of warm milk for about 30 minutes. Combine chopped walnuts with pignoli, half of the sugar, half of the orange and lemon rinds and all of the cocoa powder. Toss gently to mix thoroughly. Drain raisins and pat dry with paper toweling. Add to the nut mixture, tossing gently to mix evenly.

When sponge has doubled, melt ½ cup of the butter over a double boiler and set aside.

Pour over the sponge, one at a time, the remaining sugar, the egg yolks, the rum, the remaining grated citrus rind, and the pinch of salt. Stir everything into the sponge with a wooden spoon, then add lukewarm butter and work in all but 5 or 6 tablespoons of the flour.

Transfer dough to a wooden board and knead until the remaining flour is incorporated and the dough is smooth; this will take about 15 minutes. With a lightly floured rolling pin, roll dough out into a 9-inch rectangle, ½ inch thick.

Beat the egg whites until stiff but still shiny. Using a spatula, spread beaten whites over the sheet of dough. Sprinkle the nut filling evenly over the whites. Dot evenly with the remaining 2 tablespoons of butter. Roll the dough lengthwise, jelly-roll fashion. Butter an 11- to 12-inch pizza pan or metal pie plate. Lay the filled roll into the pan, turning it to form a ring and letting dough end overlap on the roll: press flap so it will stick to dough.

Cover the pan with a dish towel and let the dough rise for about 2 hours, or until doubled in bulk.

Preheat oven to 400° F. Bake the ring for about 40 minutes, or until the top is golden brown and the bottom of the ring sounds hollow when it is tapped. Remove from the oven and gently lift or slide the *rotolo* onto a rack to cool. This will take about 2 hours.

Serve in thick slices.

GINGERBREAD HOUSE

A good deal of the recipe testing for this book was done by Rena and Gary Coyle, the husband-and-wife team who have cooked and baked professionally at several New York restaurants and catering establishments. Mrs. Coyle's specialty is baking, and the gingerbread house below is one she used to make for the bakery at the World Trade Center's Big Kitchen. The golden-brown dough is sturdy enough to be used for gingerbread men and other cookie tree ornaments.

2¾ cups granulated sugar
1¾ cups brown sugar, firmly packed
1½ cups (¾ pound) unsalted butter
7 eggs
5 tablespoons dark molasses
1 tablespoon plus ¼ teaspoon baking soda
2 teaspoons salt
6¼ cups cake flour
1 tablespoon ginger
1 tablespoon cinnamon
1 recipe Royal Icing, page 207
Hard candies or candy confetti and sprinkles for decoration, as needed
Baker's parchment
1 gingerbread house pattern (see below)

This dough must be mixed and chilled for 12 to 24 hours before it is to be rolled out and baked.

Combine the white and brown sugars. Cream with butter until smooth, light, and fluffy. Beat eggs in one at a time, blending each in before the next is added. Stir in molasses.

Add dry ingredients and mix in gently but thoroughly. The dough should be evenly blended, but it should incorporate as little air as possible, so do not overmix. Roll in a ball, cover with waxed paper or plastic wrap, and chill for 12 to 24 hours.

Preheat the oven to 350°F.

Cover two jelly-roll pans with baker's parchment. Roll the dough out ¼ inch thick on a floured board using a floured rolling pin. Place on the parchment. Bake for 15 to 20 minutes, or until the dough is firm and begins to take on a light golden color. Remove from oven and immediately cut the gingerbread into sections, using the pattern made from the instructions below. Be sure

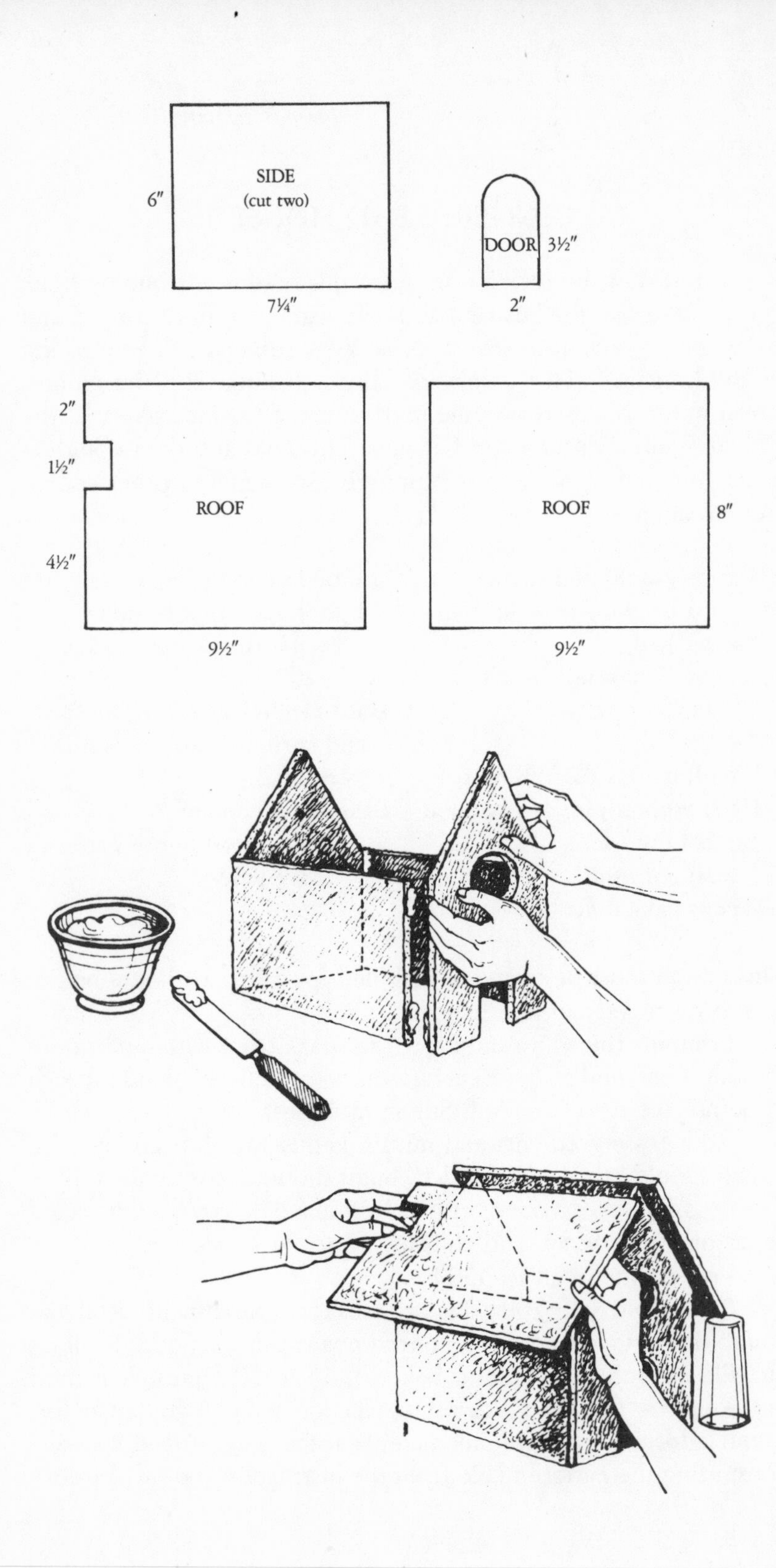
SIDE
(cut two)
6″
7¼″
DOOR
3½″
2″
2″
1½″
ROOF
4½″
9½″
ROOF
8″
9½″

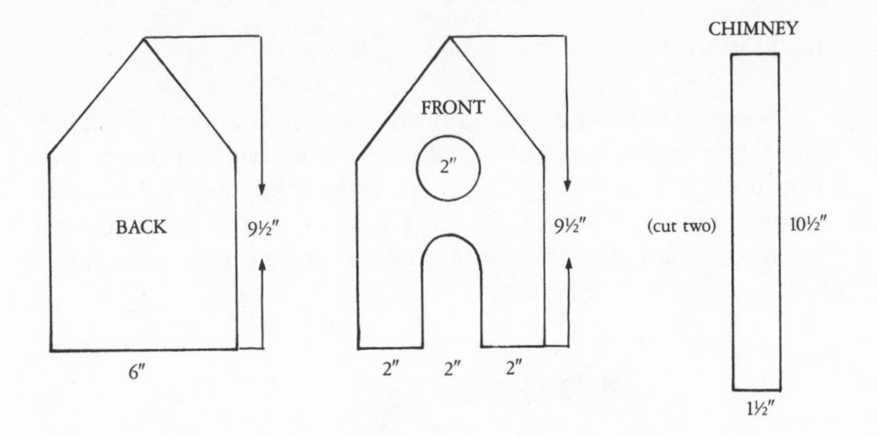

to cut duplicates of the sections as shown on the drawing. You should have 9 pieces altogether. Work quickly, or the dough will become too brittle as it cools. Pieces can be returned to oven if necessary to keep them soft enough. Place the sections on a rack to cool thoroughly before you attempt to construct the house.

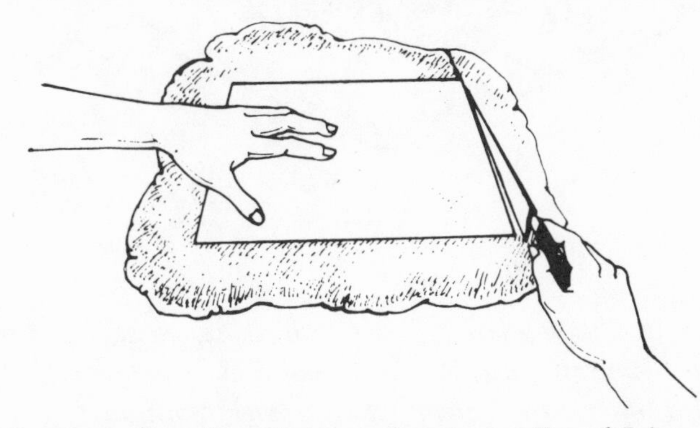

While gingerbread sections cool, prepare Royal Icing according to recipe. To construct the house, begin by working with the back and two side panel sections. Put a dab of Royal Icing on each of the back corners of the side panels. Place the panels so that they adhere to the inside corners of the back panel. Dab Royal Icing onto the front corners of the side panels. Place the front panel so that it adheres to the side panels.

Dab Royal Icing onto the peaks of the front and back panels and spread icing on one long side of the roof panel. Place the iced roof panel over one sloping side of the front and back peaks. Repeat with the second roof panel. If the roof slides down, brace the bottom edges by sliding glasses under them until the icing is set.

Assemble the chimney as shown and, when set, stick it onto the roof with Royal Icing.

(continued)

Decorate the house with icing and candies as shown. To create thin line decorations, such as outlines of windows and doors, use Royal Icing in a decorating tube. For large solid-white areas, such as snow on the roof, spread the icing with a spatula. Candy decorations can be stuck on with dabs of icing, or can be pressed onto icing decorations before they have dried.

Leon Lianides, the proprietor of The Coach House, one of New York's most impeccable restaurants, was born in Greece, and he and his wife Aphrodite still prepare the butter-rich, honey-sweet cookies traditional in that country for Christmas. The following three recipes are from their holiday repertory.

WALNUT ROLLS

- ½ pound shelled walnuts, finely chopped
- ½ teaspoon cinnamon
- ½ teaspoon powdered cloves
- ¼ cup sugar
- 18 leaves of phyllo dough
- 2 cups (1 pound) unsalted butter, melted

SYRUP:

- 2 cups water
- 1½ cups sugar
- 1 slice lemon

Preheat oven to 375°F.

Combine nuts with cinnamon, cloves, and sugar. Set aside. Brush three phyllo leaves generously with melted butter and stack them on each other evenly. Sprinkle evenly with a thin layer of the nut-sugar mixture. Brush three more sheets of dough with butter, stack them, and lay them over the nut mixture. Sprinkle another layer of nuts on the top sheet of dough.

Roll lengthwise, jelly-roll fashion. Brush top of roll with melted butter. Prepare two more rolls in this fashion, using the remaining sheets of dough and nut mixture. Cut each roll into 1-inch slices. Place the slices side by side in one or more baking pans. Bake about 30 minutes, or until the pastry is crisp and golden brown.

While walnut rolls bake, prepare the syrup. Combine water, sugar, and lemon slice in a small, heavy-bottomed saucepan and simmer for about 10 minutes, or until a light syrup is formed. Pour warm syrup over walnut rolls as soon as they are taken from the oven. Serve the cookies at room temperature. Store in airtight metal cookie tins.

Makes about 4 dozen pieces

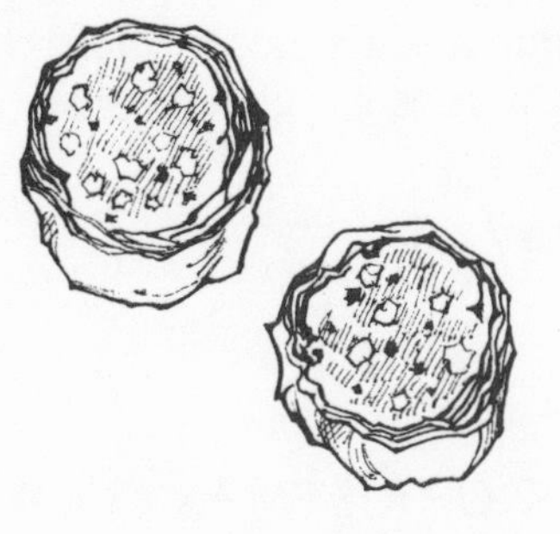

KOURAMBIEDES

These crumbly cookies, snowy with confectioners' sugar, are served at all Greek festive occasions. At Christmas they are usually studded with cloves to recall the spices the Wise Men brought to the Christ child.

(continued)

1 cup blanched almonds
2 cups (1 pound) unsalted butter
4 tablespoons confectioners' sugar
Pinch of salt
1 egg yolk
1 tablespoon Grand Marnier or brandy
4 cups cake flour
About 72 whole cloves for garnish (optional)
Confectioners' sugar, for sprinkling

Preheat oven to 450° F. Place almonds on a baking sheet or in a pie tin and roast for 7 or 8 minutes, or until they take on a pale sand color. Cool and grind very fine.

Cream butter thoroughly until it is fluffy. Combine confectioners' sugar with salt and sift the two. Gradually beat into the butter. Add egg yolk and cream well with butter-sugar mixture. Beat in Grand Marnier or brandy.

Sift cake flour and gradually stir into butter mixture with ground almonds until dough is soft, pliant, and can be rolled without sticking to your hands. If it is sticky, chill for 1 hour.

Break off rounds of dough and gently pat and shape into dome-shaped mounds, each just a little more than 1 inch in diameter. If desired, stud the center of each cookie with a whole clove. Place on an ungreased cookie sheet and bake until they are a pale sand color, about 20 minutes. Do not let these cookies brown. Cool on racks. Sift confectioners' sugar generously over the cooled cookies.

Makes about 6 dozen cookies

GREEK CHRISTMAS COOKIES

1 cup (½ pound) unsalted butter, at room temperature
½ cup confectioners' sugar
1 extra-large egg
¼ cup heavy cream
2 tablespoons brandy or Grand Marnier
3 cups flour, sifted
½ teaspoon salt
1 teaspoon baking powder
1 egg yolk beaten with 1 teaspoon cold water
½ cup sesame seeds
Candied red cherries, cut in strips

Preheat oven to 350°F.

Cream butter with sugar until the mixture is very light and fluffy. This should take about 10 minutes in an electric mixer. Add the egg, heavy cream, and brandy or Grand Marnier and beat thoroughly, allowing about 5 minutes in an electric mixer.

Resift flour with salt and baking powder, and, using a wooden spoon, slowly and gradually blend it into the butter mixture until you have a soft dough. Test the mixture in the palm of your hand to see if it rolls easily without sticking. It should be soft and pliant. Add flour if dough is too sticky.

Cut dough into small portions and roll each into a ball about the size of a walnut. Working between your hands, roll out each ball to form a thin rope about 16 inches long. Bend the rope in half and twist it into a coil. Turn it into a wreath. Let the ends of each wreath overlap and press gently to secure.

Brush wreaths with beaten egg yolk. Sprinkle generously with sesame seeds and decorate with a cherry strip at the top of each wreath.

Arrange the wreaths on an ungreased cookie sheet and bake for about 20 minutes, or until cookies are light golden.

Remove from baking sheet and cool on rack.

Makes about 3 dozen cookies

KENTUCKY PECAN BOURBON CAKE

Charles Patteson, a friend who is expert at cooking the specialties of his native Kentucky, prepares this solid bourbon-scented fruitcake each year.

2 cups (1 pound) unsalted butter
2½ cups granulated sugar
10 extra-large eggs
1 cup bourbon whiskey
2 whole nutmegs, freshly grated
3½ cups all-purpose flour
About 1 pound (or a 15-ounce box) white raisins
¼ pound citron, diced
1½ pounds shelled pecans, coarsely chopped

Preheat oven to 250°F. Butter two loaf pans, each 9 × 5 × 3½. Line the bottom and sides of each with strips of waxed paper or baker's parchment and butter the top side of the paper. Set aside.

Cream butter and sugar until light and fluffy. Beat eggs lightly and gradually pour into sugar-butter mixture, mixing well between additions. Stir in bourbon. Add nutmeg and flour and blend in. Stir in raisins, citron, and nuts. Turn into prepared pans and bake for 4 hours, or until a tester inserted into the center of the cake comes out clean.

Let cake cool in pan. This will taste best if it is allowed to ripen 24 hours to 1 week before it is cut. The completely cool cake can be wrapped in foil and stored in a cool room or in the refrigerator. For a more pronounced bourbon flavor, soak a length of new cheesecloth in the whiskey, then wrap the wrung-out cloth around the cake. Wrap with foil and store in a cool place. Peel back only as much paper as needed to cut the slices you want for each serving. This keeps in the freezer or refrigerator for months. It is best cut into slices of just a little less than ½ inch thick.

Makes 1 or 2 loaf cakes weighing about 6 pounds

Variations: Brandy or any whiskey you prefer can be substituted for bourbon.

A half-and-half combination of pecans and black walnuts may be used.

Délices La Côte Basque, one of New York's newer patisseries, has been enjoying popularity almost from the moment its doors were opened. The reason is its owner, Guy Pascal, who turns out richly intricate pastries as well as intriguing savories, all of which are served in the café section of his bakery. The two recipes that follow are for Christmas specialties which Mr. Pascal cherishes from his childhood in Provence.

COLOMBIER

Essentially a nut torte with an almost frothy lightness, these thin, airy cakes may be used in layers with whipped cream or butter-cream fillings. Traditionally, the cake is eaten plain, and though coffee is the French preference, it would be especially appropriate with tea.

8 eggs, separated
1 tablespoon water
1 cup granulated sugar
8 ounces almond flour (page 242)
¾ cup Kirsch
Grated rind of 2 oranges
2 teaspoons vanilla extract
Pinch of salt
2 ounces sliced almonds
Butter and flour for pans

Preheat the oven to 300°F.

Butter two 9-inch round layer-cake pans. Sprinkle the inside of each with flour and tap out excess. Set aside.

Combine egg yolks with water and sugar in the top of a double boiler. Set over the lower pan half-filled with scalding but not boiling water. Beat the yolks and sugar until very light, pale, and puffy.

Pour egg mixture into a bowl and gradually stir in the almond flour, mixing well between additions. Stir in kirsch, orange rind, and vanilla.

Beat egg whites with a pinch of salt until they stand in stiff but shiny peaks. Stir 2 or 3 tablespoons of egg white into the yolk mixture, then carefully but thoroughly fold in the remaining whites, using a rubber spatula.

Divide the batter between the two prepared cake pans. Sprinkle the top of each lightly with half of the sliced almonds. Bake for

1 hour. The cake will sink slightly in the middle when removed from the oven. Let it cool in the pan before moving.

Makes 2 nine-inch round layer cakes

Note: If you prefer one large cake, use a 12-inch round layer-cake pan.

GIBASSIERS

- ½ ounce cake yeast or 1 package of dry yeast
- 1 teaspoon sugar
- ¼ cup warm water
- ½ cup (¼ pound) melted unsalted butter
- 2¼ cups cake flour or as needed, plus extra for rolling dough
- ½ cup granulated sugar
- 2 eggs
- Grated rind of 2 oranges
- Grated rind of 2 lemons
- 1 egg beaten with 1 tablespoon milk

If using cake yeast, mash with the 1 teaspoon of sugar and stir into the warm water. If using dry yeast, sprinkle with the 1 teaspoon sugar on top of the warm water. Set aside in a warm corner for 5 to 10 minutes, or until the mixture begins to froth.

Mix together the melted butter, 2 cups flour, and sugar. Stir in the yeast, eggs, and citrus rinds. Mix until well blended. Cover the bowl loosely with a cloth and set the dough in a warm, draft-free corner to rise for 1 hour or until doubled in bulk.

Preheat the oven to 400°F.

Punch the dough down. Sprinkle flour on a board or wooden counter top and rub some flour onto a rolling pin. Gradually work in up to ¼ cup additional flour, or until dough is still sticky but workable. Turn dough out onto floured surface and roll to 1 inch thickness. With a sharp, pointed knife, cut the dough into the shape of a five-pointed star. If you like, you can use the cardboard star pattern described on page 219. Trimmings from the dough can be cut with cookie cutters. Place star carefully on a cookie sheet and brush top with egg wash. Bake for about 20 minutes, or until top is pale golden-brown. Let cool before serving.

Dieter Schorner, the German-born pastry chef at the New York French restaurant Le Chantilly, is one of the three or four most talented bakers in the country. The following five Christmas specialties are among his childhood favorites. The one exception is an antique recipe from Padua, Italy, for the soft macaroons known as Amaretti.

Bitter almonds, the authentic ingredient in these cookies, are rarely available, so Dieter Schorner substituted plain almonds and almond extract.

AMARETTI

½ pound (1½ cups) sliced blanched almonds
3 cups granulated sugar
¾ to 1 cup egg whites, lightly beaten
Grated rind of 1 lemon
2 teaspoons almond extract
1 teaspoon vanilla extract
Confectioners' sugar

Grind almonds very fine in a food processor. Add sugar and continue grinding to a paste. Add half the egg whites gradually to form a thick, smooth paste that holds a shape. Add grated lemon rind and almond extract and let mix for a second.

Turn into an electric mixer and, using the flat paddle at medium speed, beat in enough of the remaining egg white to produce a thick fluff—this will take about 5 minutes.

Butter and flour two or more large baking sheets. Using a pastry bag with a #2 tube, or two teaspoons, form macaroons, each about 1 to 1½ inches across. Leave a 1-inch space between each macaroon. Sprinkle generously with confectioner's sugar. Let stand for 4 to 5 hours or overnight, uncovered, in a cool corner. They will become thin and round.

Preheat oven to 400°F. Pinch each cookie in on all sides, toward the center, to thicken. Bake 10 to 15 minutes, just until the macaroons begin to turn a pale golden color. Do not overbake or they will lose their chewiness. Cool on a rack. When cold, store in an airthight container in the refrigerator.

Makes about 4 dozen

COCONUT MACAROONS

2½ cups granulated sugar
2⅓ cups (8 ounces) shredded, fresh unsweetened coconut (see note)
1 cup egg whites (whites of about 6 extra-large eggs)
1 teaspoon vanilla extract
⅓ cup plus 2 tablespoons all-purpose flour
Baker's parchment paper

Preheat oven to 350°F.

Butter a baking sheet and cover it with parchment paper. Combine sugar, coconut, and egg whites in the top of a double boiler and stir. Set over the lower half of the double boiler with hot water and heat until mixture reaches 170°F. on a candy thermometer. Remove from heat and stir in vanilla and flour.

Spoon into a pastry bag and, without any nozzle, pipe macaroons about 1½ inches in diameter onto parchment paper, leaving about 1 inch between each. Two teaspoons may be used if you have no pastry bag. Bake for 15 minutes or until macaroons begin to turn pale gold.

Remove from parchment, cool on a rack, and store in an airtight container. These will keep for several weeks in a cool place.

Makes about 3 dozen

Note: Shredded, fresh unsweetened coconut can be purchased in health-food stores.

SPITZKUCHEN

1¾ cups dark honey
½ cup water
7 tablespoons unsalted butter
2½ tablespoons baking soda
1 teaspoon each allspice, mace, cinnamon, and nutmeg
½ teaspoon powdered ginger
2¾ cups all-purpose flour
3 cups rye flour
1¾ cups currants
¾ cup finely chopped candied orange rind
2 ounces semisweet baking chocolate

Preheat oven to 400°F.

Combine honey, water, and butter in a heavy-bottomed saucepan. Slowly heat to the boiling point. Pour into a mixing bowl. Sift together the baking soda, spices, and both flours and stir into the honey mixture. Fold in the currants and orange rind and mix until the dough is smooth, pliable, and not sticky, adding a little more flour if needed.

Shape dough into long sausage rolls, about 1 inch in diameter. The length is not too important but depends on what is easy for you to handle. Two or three rolls would be about right for this amount of dough. Place rolls on a lightly buttered baking sheet and bake for about 10 to 15 minutes. Melt the chocolate. It should not be warmer than 90°F. Brush onto the rolls. Let cool on the pan and cut into diagonal pieces, each about 1 inch long, as shown.

Makes about 10 dozen

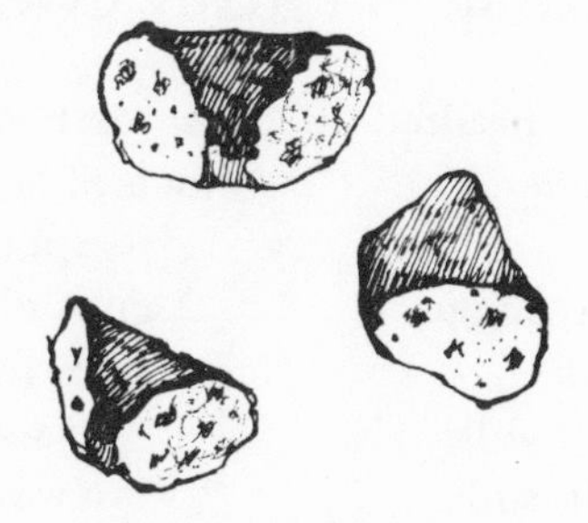

OATMEAL COOKIES

"When we were children at home, it was our dream to eat these simple cookies warm from the oven," Dieter Schorner said. Try them after only a few minutes of cooling.

- **1½ cups (¾ pound) unsalted butter**
- **1 cup granulated sugar**
- **1 teaspoon vanilla extract**
- **2 teaspoons sifted baking soda**
- **2¾ cups Quaker's old-fashioned oatmeal**
- **2⅓ cups all-purpose flour**
- **1½ cups raisins**

Preheat oven to 375°F. Butter a cookie sheet and line with baker's parchment. Cream butter and sugar until light and fluffy. Stir in vanilla. Add sifted baking soda and stir in. Add oatmeal, flour, and raisins and stir in thoroughly. Mix well. Using your hands, form dough into balls, each just a little larger than a walnut. Place them about 1 inch apart on parchment-lined cookie sheet. Bake 20 to 25 minutes or until pale golden brown. Remove from paper and cool on rack. Although delicious when warm, these are really meant to be eaten cold. Pack in an airtight container when they have cooled completely.

Makes about 5 dozen

CINNAMON-RAISIN COOKIES

- **1½ cups (¾ pound) unsalted butter, at room temperature**
- **1 cup dark brown sugar, firmly packed**
- **2 eggs, plus 1 egg yolk**
- **1 teaspoon baking soda**
- **1 teaspoon cinnamon**
- **⅛ teaspoon nutmeg**
- **⅛ teaspoon ginger**
- **Pinch of salt**
- **1 teaspoon vanilla extract**
- **2 cups all-purpose flour**
- **1½ cups finely ground or granulated unblanched hazelnuts**
- **1 cup raisins**

ICING:

2 cups confectioners' sugar
¼ cup water
1 tablespoon light rum

Preheat oven to 425°F. Butter a cookie sheet and line with parchment paper. Cream butter and sugar until light and fluffy. Add whole eggs and yolk, and cream into the butter-sugar mixture. Combine baking soda, spices, and salt and sift into butter-sugar-egg mixture. Add vanilla and mix well. Add flour and nuts and stir in gently until well blended. Stir in raisins.

Using a pastry bag without a nozzle, pipe out sausagelike rolls of dough onto paper. Or shape long, thin rolls (about ½ inch in diameter) with your hands and place them on the parchment. Flatten tops with tines of a fork as shown. Bake about 15 minutes.

While dough bakes, mix confectioners' sugar, water, and rum. Brush icing on the rolls of dough when removed from oven. Let cool and cut in ½-inch diagonal slices as shown.

Makes about 8 dozen

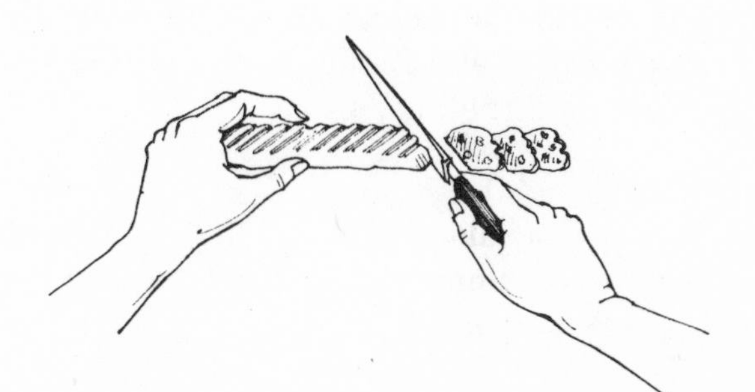

André Soltner, chef-propriétaire *of Lutèce, which is one of this country's finest French restaurants, is a native of Alsace, a fact that probably accounts for his unusual talents as both chef and* pâtissier. *The following two recipes are traditional Alsatian specialties baked each Christmas by Mr. Soltner's mother.*

ALSATIAN "SCHWOWEBRETTLE," OR PETITS FOURS DE NOËL

1 cup (½ pound) unsalted butter
1 cup granulated sugar
¼ teaspoon cinnamon
2⅓ cups almond flour (see page 242)
Grated rind of ½ lemon
2 large egg yolks
3 to 4 cups sifted all-purpose flour
1 egg yolk beaten with 1 teaspoon cold water

Dough should be prepared about 12 hours before it is to be baked.

Knead the butter until it is soft and pliant, but not greasy. Add sugar, cinnamon, almond flour, lemon rind, and 2 egg yolks. Gradually work in flour, either kneading by hand or with the dough hook of an electric mixer. Work in just enough flour to give you a firm, homogenous mass. If dough is too crumbly, work in a little extra egg yolk. Wrap in plastic or place in plastic bag and chill overnight.

Preheat oven to 350°F. Butter a cookie sheet.

Cut dough into convenient pieces to work with. Lightly flour a pastry board and rolling pin, and roll dough out to a thickness of ⅛ inch. Using cutters that are about 1½ to 2 inches across, cut out star, club, heart, and Christmas shapes. Press scraps together and reroll.

Place cut-out cookies on cookie sheet. Brush with egg wash and bake for 10 to 12 minutes. Cool on rack and store in airtight tin. Keep in a cool, dry place.

Makes about 7 dozen cookies

BIREWECHE (ALSATIAN PEAR BREAD)

- ¼ pound prunes
- ¼ pound dried pears
- ¼ pound dried figs
- 2 ounces light sultana raisins
- 2 ounces black sultana raisins
- 1 ounce unblanched hazelnuts, coarsely chopped
- 1 ounce blanched almonds, coarsely chopped
- 1 ounce walnuts, coarsely chopped
- ¼ cup sugar
- 1 cup Kirsch
- Pinch each of nutmeg and cinnamon
- ½ pound Basic Bread Dough (page 240)
- Butter for pan
- 1 egg yolk beaten with 1 teaspoon cold water

The fruit filling should be prepared the night before the bread is to be baked.

Cook prunes and pears in just enough water to cover them for a few minutes, or until they are just soft enough to cut easily. Cut prunes in strips, discarding pits. Cut pears and figs in strips. Wash raisins under running cold water and add to cut fruits along with nuts, sugar, kirsch, and spices. Mix well and let stand at room temperature, loosely covered, overnight.

Prepare bread dough as described below. Let it rise once. Punch down and slowly, carefully knead fruit into dough until well distributed. Shape into a long loaf and place on a buttered baking sheet.

Preheat oven to 350°F.

Let shaped bread rise, loosely covered, for about 30 minutes. Brush with egg wash and bake for 1 hour. The flavor will develop to its fullest if this bread is not cut for 24 hours after it is baked. When cool, wrap it in plastic or foil. It will keep for weeks. Serve thinly sliced.

Makes 1 two-pound loaf

BASIC BREAD DOUGH

1 package dry yeast
1½ cups cool water
2 to 3 cups bread flour
1 teaspoon salt

Sprinkle yeast into a large bowl and add 1½ cups cool water; set in a warm corner for about 5 minutes. Beat in 2 cups of flour and salt, using the beater of an electric mixer if you have one. Beat until the batter is smooth and pulls away cleanly from sides of bowl. Beat in as much of the remaining cup of flour as the batter will take. Knead for 5 minutes, using the dough hook of an electric mixer, or knead about 10 minutes by hand. Dough should be smooth and slightly blistered.

Place dough in a lightly greased bowl, cover loosely, and set in a warm, draft-free corner until doubled in bulk. This will take about 1½ hours. At this point, combine with fruits as described above.

Makes about ½ pound of dough

Variations: German Pear Bread or Kutzelbrot is made much the same way, but usually 2 tablespoons chopped candied fruit peel would be added to the fruit mixture, as would a few drops of rosewater.

Styrian Kletzenbrot is made in the same way, but pumpernickel dough is substituted for the white bread dough.

THE CHRISTMAS PANTRY SHELF

Chapter Ten

Following is a list and explanation of a few special ingredients needed for Christmas recipes in this book:

Almond Flour: This consists of finely pulverized blanched almonds. It is available in some health food stores and all bakery supply houses. It can be bought or ordered by mail from Paprikas Weiss, 1546 Second Avenue, New York, NY 10028. It is also available at H. Roth & Sons, 1577 First Avenue, New York, NY 10028. Haddar brand almond flour is distributed by Erba Food Products, 624 Court Street, Brooklyn, NY 11231.

Almond Paste and Marzipan: See pages 164–165.

Bakers' Rice Wafers: These thin white translucent wafers are used as a base and topping for many cookies and candies. They may be purchased from a bakers' supply house or a neighborhood bakery, if you order them in advance. They usually come in sheets and you cut them to the shapes you want. They are also used as communion wafers in church services, and especially decorative ones (Oplatekt) are given to Polish families by their priests to be eaten at home on Christmas Eve, or Wigilia.

Cake Flour: This is very fine wheat flour. It is available in supermarkets, where Swansdown is the brand most commonly found. It is also available at bakery supply houses and in many health food shops, where whole wheat cake flour is sold. If unavailable, use a half-and-half combination of all-purpose flour and cornstarch to make the total amount of cake flour called for.

Candied Cherries and Fruit Peel: Red and green cherries, citron, orange, lemon and angelica can be purchased in whole pieces or diced. Store in airtight containers away from heat so that they do not become dry or sticky. Buy large pieces to cut into decorations for tops of cakes.

Coconut Milk: To make this, you need fresh coconuts, or if you can get it, freshly grated unsweetened coconut meat. Cover 2 cups grated coconut meat with 6 cups boiling water. Let stand for 30 minutes; then strain off milk, squeezing the coconut as dry as possible. Discard coconut meat. Makes 6 cups. Coconut milk is sometimes sold, already prepared, in Latin-American grocery stores. Canned coconut cream, a product similar to sweetened condensed milk, can sometimes be substituted (page 153).

Colored Sugar: To sprinkle on tops of cookies and cakes that are plain or iced.

Glacéed Fruits: Pineapple, pears, apricots, figs, etc., are usually purchased in large pieces. Use chopped in cakes and puddings, or in larger pieces for top decorations on cakes.

Nuts: Nuts purchased in the shell are preferable to those already shelled as they are more likely to be fresh. Do not buy shelled nuts without trying a few to see if they have become rencid. At best, shelled nuts should be stored in the refrigerator, as they are in many health food stores. Vacuum-packed nuts are generally softened in texture and musty in flavor. If you must use them, let them air for 10 or 15 minutes after the can is opened; it is also a good idea to freshen them in a low oven (about 250°) for 10 minutes.

If you buy unshelled nuts, you will need a little more than twice the amount called for in shelled nuts. To get on pound of shelled walnuts or almonds, buy about 2½ pounds. The exact amount varies somewhat with the moisture in the nut and the variety; paper-thin Italian almonds have lighter shells than those from California. Pecan shells are somewhat lighter than those of walnuts but there is more waste because they are delicate and hard to crack. It is best to weigh shelled nuts on a small kitchen scale.

Oblaten Wafers: Also known as *gaufrettes,* these are crisp brown pastry wafers used as a base for candies and cookies. (We know them best as the crackers used for Nabisco wafers.) They come in large, round flat tins, and in smaller wedge shapes or squares, and can be purchased in gourmet food shops of department stores, or in German neighborhoods, where they are known as Karlsbad Oblaten.

Paper Cookie Stickers: You'll find these in German and Eastern European grocery stores and bakeries during the Christmas season.

They are colorful cutouts with pictures of Santa Claus, trees, wreaths, etc. They are to be stuck onto the plain or iced surface of cookies, such as Lebkuchen, pages 89–90, and Meringues, page 98, which are then hung on the tree or used to fill children's stockings. Place stickers on warm or freshly iced cookies so they will stick.

Paper and Parchment: In many Christmas recipes for breads and pound cakes, either brown paper or parchment is called for. Their use is interchangeable. If you can get white bakers' parchment, its use is preferable to brown paper. If you use the latter, be sure it is very clean and has no chemical odor.

Poppy Seeds: Since these contain oil, they become rancid with age, so be sure those you use are fresh. Instructions for washing and grinding them are included where necessary in specific recipes. They can sometimes be purchased already ground from Hungarian grocery stores, but be even doubly sure they are fresh.

Spices: Cinnamon, nutmeg, cloves, allspice, mace, ginger, cardamom, anise, pepper and other spices are used in the Christmas recipes of all countries. Whether you grind your own or buy them already ground, be sure they are as fresh as possible for maximum flavor.

Sugar Sprinkles (Confetti): These are multicolored tiny candies which are usually available in Italian grocery stores and bakeries, but can also be found in some supermarkets. Jordan almonds are often included.

Index